LIBERATE YOURSELF:

YOUR PAST IS NOT YOUR PRISON.

The key to finding happiness, light, and success

LUZ AVILA-KYNCL

Salud con Luz
www.saludconluz.com

Copyright © 2017 by Luz Esther Kyncl

ISBN 978-0-9992139-0-2
eISBN 978-0-9992139-1-9
Library of congress number - 2017949370

The author of this book is not a physician, and the ideas and suggestions in this book are not intended as a substitute for the medical advice of a trained health professional. Consult your physician before adopting the suggestions in this book, as well as about any condition that may require diagnosis or medical attention.

CONTENTS

Dedication

To God, for being the guide of my life.

To my daughters, Isabella and Adriana, for being the incentive to keep going.

To my husband, Robert, for being my unconditional support.

To my mother, for being an example of perseverance in life.

INTRODUCTION

I wrote the first lines of this book when I was headed to Japan, ready to celebrate my fortieth birthday with my husband, a prominent business executive. I was also lovingly admiring my daughters, two of the most blessed girls I know. The first-class cabin seemed surreal... just like my whole life did. What would the lonely, sad, poor girl I once was but left behind think of all this? I wish today that I could hug that unwanted girl who grew up literally eating dirt in a slum of the Dominican Republic.

My life today isn't perfect, but I am perfectly happy: a professional woman, mother, and wife who gets up healthy every morning, with a vivid smile and an eagerness to live her life. I freed myself from the prison of my past, and now I want to help you do the same. Who told you that you can't be happy? Who told you that you can't be loved, beautiful, healthy, successful, and the owner of an endless peace? Liberate yourself from what your family, bosses, "friends," or even you yourself have told you or made you feel in the past. I guarantee you that you can do it; you have the right to be infinitely happy, regardless of where you come from or the obstacles that you face today.

I can humbly tell you that I feel proud of being able to positively influence my clients' lives with messages that inspire and motivate, utilizing guides of nutrition and empowerment, in addition to one or two experiences of my own story when appropriate. Throughout the years, together we have achieved wonderful changes that have pointed them in the right direction toward a better future. That´s why today, in my 40s, I've decided to write this book, as I have the desire to help other people from a broad and inclusive perspective. I have lived through the process of coming out of my personal prison, and the words printed in this book have been born from my inspiration and my own experience. I´m not speaking just to speak or to exclusively express literary or academic knowledge of my professional training; I speak from the deep understanding that such transformation does exist, and it changes destinies. My clients and I are the tangible proof that a sad or difficult past does not dictate the future; on the contrary, such a past is a medal of honor as we look for happiness with more eagerness and transform ourselves with more instruments. You see, living in the past creates a lot of difficulties in our present and future lives. When we don´t heal the wounds of yesterday, the pain, disappointment, unhealthy relationships, and bad habits condemn us to a mental, emotional, and physical prison. Every day the loneliness, depression, obesity, addiction, violence, and stress indicators grow, and few people can find the key that frees them from an existence plagued by unhappiness. However, this imprisonment is only ours if we allow it to be. The decisions that we make today can keep us in that prison for life or free us forever, allowing us to finally find light, happiness, and success.

This guide to build a healthy and successful life, "PlanPluz," has been written with energy and positive and healing vibes so that everyone who reads it will benefit from every word. With this book, I want to broaden the reader's knowledge about how to recover and maintain wellness and good health through a physical, spiritual, and emotional guide that includes the nutrition of both body and soul, in a practical way. I advise my readers to read it from beginning to end, without skipping any paragraphs, in order to obtain maximum benefit. I hope that my words reach a wide audience, regardless of the level of academic or intellectual knowledge that each one has; thus, in the pages of this book, you will find theoretical and practical information narrated in a simple and straightforward way.

Somebody said that the right mentor or information comes to us when we are prepared and willing to receive it, which is why you shouldn't take this reading as a coincidence. If you are reading this, you have already taken the first step, and this book will be a door that opens itself before you towards a change—a threshold that you are now ready to cross.

If much of the information that I am about to give you sounds familiar, it is because you already know it deep within yourself and are conscious of these principles, even if you still might not be aware of it. We all have an innate knowledge that extends beyond all academic studies that we have undertaken. This knowledge accompanies us all throughout our lives, and when we are ready to put it into action, it is revealed to us in some way or another. Mostly the answers that we seek so ardently are very simple. In fact, it is in simplicity that the great masters of history have found illumination. This is why the help that I here offer lacks complexities.

This book will help you to become conscious of you own emotional, mental, and physical struggles and will encourage you to change those patterns that keep you locked in the dungeon of unhappiness. It is an honest call and an inspiring and practical guide from a woman, mother, and health professional for you to take responsibility for your actual condition as a twenty-first-century human being who can be entirely happy. It also teaches, proves, and explains that we are not victims of our past and that only we have the power and responsibility to mold our future. I hope you enjoy it!

"Don´t let your past, whatever it is, obscure your vision of a bright future." – Alex Rovira

CHAPTER 1

Nice to meet you, I´m Luz.

I would like to begin this chapter by thanking and honoring my past, which for many years I perceived as a prison; nevertheless, it was the blessing that allowed me to become the healthy, happy woman, mother, and professional I now am.

My story begins in a slum of La Romana in the Dominican Republic, where I was born and raised in a household that was filled with despair and suffered from material and emotional scarcity. I lived with both of my parents, my two brothers, my sister, and some close family with whom we shared a single bathroom outside of the house. Of my early childhood, I only have scattered memories, given that in our family there were no pictures, nor the desire to save memories. There were also very few celebrations. Birthdays and weddings were alien to our life experience, and the only parties to which we paid some attention were Christmas and the Three Kings Day. I grew almost without belongings, and once each year, for Three Kings Day, I received a humble toy that never met my expectations. Instead of receiving the beautiful Barbie doll that I had dreamt of, I was given a "knock off" version that ended up breaking after a few weeks, making me even sadder and disappointed for the loss. In my house, as in the whole neighborhood, the struggle for daily survival prevailed, and any longing for improvement was decimated by the limits imposed by poverty and the violence that emerges from daily suffering. Our basic needs weren´t met, and the educational and cultural offerings were very minimal, especially for my mother who, because of her limited education through only the third grade, was always ridiculed and judged by my father´s family. Indeed, the women in the neighborhood dealt daily with a male-dominated society where the mere fact of being a female was a sentence of devaluation, gender violence, and sexual abuse. Aggressiveness and prostitution were a part of the routine in the streets of my neighborhood, and the lack of social security and basic healthcare were the reality of our daily lives.

One of my deepest memories is of the eyes of my father, one of which was normal, and one of which was made of glass. This gave him a deformed and grotesque appearance that caused me to feel a strange mixture of sadness and fear when I looked at him. There were times when my father took out the glass eye to clean it, leaving his face with an unsightly, puckered hole. It was as if there were a void in what is supposed to represent the window of the soul. I must have been around five or six years old when I confronted the face of my father, with only one eye, holding the other one in his hand. When my father looked at me with only one eye, I felt confused and horrified. I wanted to cure him, but I didn´t have the instruments.

My mother´s eyes were different; they were filled with sadness, resentment, and rejection towards me, an aversion that I only understood years later when I overheard her say that she never wanted to have "hens." Unfortunately, that wish wasn't fulfilled, and after her first boy, my sister and I were born. Her fourth child was my younger brother, who signified the return of blessings to my family. My mother always loved her sons, and she stayed with my father even if he humiliated and abused her, perhaps because of the saying, it's "better to have known evil than unknown good." I have never talked to her about this issue, but I think that she endured so much misery with my father because deep down she was afraid to end up on the streets, alone and with nothing. After all, the house where we lived belonged to my father´s family, and the

3

act of leaving her husband would´ve been shameful and condemned by society.

Even before marrying my father, my mother was used to burdens and bitterness. She was born into a family of very poor farmers, and when she was a few months old, she was left motherless. Her father and her little brothers worked in the countryside, so she had to drop out of primary school to join the rest of the family. When my grandfather remarried, my mother also had to help raise her new siblings. Her suffering then continued into marriage. When my father lost his eye (I never really knew the details of that loss because I never dared to ask), he was fired from his job as a policeman. His physical impairment and his lack of other skills impeded him from getting a new job. Depression and financial hardship led him to seek shelter in drink and physical and verbal family abuse as an escape mechanism for his bitterness.

My mother, once again, was forced to increase her work at the factory, and I also had to go to work. As a little girl, I went out to deliver vegetables very early at dawn before going to school. In the morning before my delivery route was the only time that I saw my mother until late at night when she got home, utterly exhausted from the long hours of labor. This was when I was literally "eating dirt," not in the metaphorical sense but in the real one, for I had an eating disorder that I only later came to understand. The disorder is known as Pica, and it consists of consuming non-nurturing substances, like ice, chalk, glue, and dirt, among other things. The causes of this disease are unknown, but it is believed that they could be related to a deprivation of love and nurturing that leads to poor or limited communication between parents and children. Children then develop a feeling of inferiority that drives them to adopt harmful attitudes about their health in order to seek attention and demand protection and support. In some less frequent occasions, Pica may be related to an inadequate diet and childhood malnutrition that motivates the body to look for the nutrients that it needs in unusual substances. During that time I didn´t know why I did it, but I remember that the act of eating dirt helped me to calm my fears and somehow cope with the stress of my daily problems.

I grew up in material and emotional poverty, but even if I wasn´t aware of it back then, I was spiritually very rich. Perhaps because of the name that my parents gave me or perhaps because of an inborn knowledge, I always had faith in the existence of a "light" at the end of the tunnel. In this first stage of my life, however, I still hadn´t seen it. My tunnel was long, dark, and seemingly endless, but somewhere in my soul, I felt that there was a power much greater than me that cared for and protected me. I had a God and with Him came faith and hope in a future that I didn't even dare to hope for, but that I secretly allowed myself to dream of. Even so, I never had the fortune that other kids have of being able to unleash my imagination. I was afraid that others would find out that I longed to get out of there, and then they would mock me and my stupid ideas. They would've laughed at my dreams of obtaining a higher education that contributed to making this world a better place, and of having an existence wherein mere day-to-day survival wouldn't be the standard. When you grow up plagued by fear, uncertainty, and emotional and physical scarcity, all you can expect is for life to hit you once and again at the turn of every corner. Thinking that "everything is going to turn out wrong" is embedded in your blood, and the predisposition to accept that you are never going to have a happy and abundant life turns into a rule accepted by everyone around you. It is then that we start building our own prisons, which can be physical, emotional, mental, or a combination of all three, as actually happens more often than not. Even though external circumstances seem to have conspired to lead us to failure, the key to escape, even if we can't believe it, is within ourselves, and the key point is maintaining our faith and our goals despite the challenges.

Alas, my life went on without major changes, and I

sunk more and more into daily misery until, during the first years of my adolescence, my mother was hired as a housekeeper by a prominent French family that took her to live and work in New York. My brothers and I stayed in La Romana with my father and his family, including uncles, aunts, and even my own grandmother, none of who ever paid us any attention. I felt inconsolably invisible when I wasn´t reminded that I was an obstacle. My father, finding himself without a wife and without a job, took out his frustration by getting drunk, being with women, and physical abusing my brothers and me. We were practically alone at home and without any supervision. I don´t recall receiving any specific display of affection or care from my father´s relatives, except by some aunt or uncle who every now and then bothered to come see how we were. Maybe they felt sorry for us, or maybe they felt remorse about being witnesses of the conditions in which my brothers and I were growing up. However, none of these feelings ever made them do anything to change our lives or save us from the abuse that we received from our father each day. On the contrary, they participated in the verbal and physical abuse that was already so familiar to us.

Despite the chaos that I was brought up in, there is something that I do thank my grandmother for: she introduced me to church, which was the only place where I felt safe and at peace. I remember that I enjoyed seeing clean, well-dressed people and listening to sermons where faith and love were exalted. Faith and love: two words that fed my light starved soul. Maybe it was there, in those moments of relief when I finally allowed myself to fill my lungs with air and let go of the sorrow, that my faith in God started to grow. At church, I learned how to pray and ask for help because, as the priest said every Sunday, "God listens to all of your prayers and all of your requests. Ask and it will be given."

Four years went by before I saw my mother again. It was 1989, and she had finally filled out the immigration paperwork and requested us from the Dominican Republic. My brothers and I arrived in New York on a warm summer night, without any belongings and minimum luggage: a bag with a few clothes, but no toys or pictures or memories of any kind because, as I mentioned earlier, we had none of that. Our baggage was mainly hopes and dreams.

The trip itself had been a real experience. It was the first time that I had traveled on a plane and the first time that I had left my town. I remember that my brothers and I couldn't believe that they offered us food and drinks on the plane. Not only that, but they also asked us if we wanted chicken or beef! We could even choose between different types of sodas and juices, tea and coffee! On that flight, I never could have imagined that in a near future, I would travel the world overwhelmed by happiness and love, feeling like the most blessed queen in the world.

In the "first world," we often forget the great significance that these basic elements, which we take for granted, have for other people. The privilege of being able to choose what to eat or drink is something that evades people's most vivid imaginations in other parts of the world. Indeed, choice can be a luxury item.

So, with my feet firmly at JFK International Airport, I felt alive and thankful for the huge opportunity that destiny was offering us, and, even if the depression and low self-esteem always followed me, I had already freed myself from abuse and family mistreatment that had marked my childhood. I embraced this escape from a life of scarcity, misery, abuse, and despair with a wonderful faith. This journey alone was a huge response to my requests for help, and I thanked God, even if many hard moments still awaited me. Travelling to the United States, especially for a person with such low income, is often an unreachable dream, and yet here we were.

Visas had miraculously materialized, which would never

had happened if my mother had not made the decision to accept that work proposal that she was offered and that separated her from us for four years. I had previously met some people in the Dominican Republic who had traveled to the United States as illegal immigrants. When they came back to visit, all of them had or pretended to have money, so I had gotten used to the idea that when I arrived at New York, I would also be rich. I arrived hungry and thirsty for everything: food, drink, culture, education, prosperity, and happiness. The first thing that fascinated me was the abundance of light. In La Romana the power went out frequently, and in New York there were so many bright lights and all of them worked perfectly. The fascination and the illusion dissipated quickly, however, when my mother was suddenly jobless, as her employers moved back to France. So, soon after our arrival we went to live in a small, shared one-room apartment in Washington Heights, where armed robbery, drug trafficking, and "low life" were the order of the day.

While I was used to cramped coexistence at home, this was the first time that I had to share my space with strangers. In adolescence, privacy starts to become important, so I was often embarrassed and uncomfortable. Nevertheless, I was still thankful for being able to live in the United States, and I was full of expectations. Food was abundant, and opportunities were also endless. All of this gave me the motivation to keep going, despite having to endure the difficulties of being a poor immigrant. Many times, I walked the streets with the illusion of finding money because in La Romana they had told me that in the U.S., abundance was so immense that you could even find dollars lying on the sidewalk. Well, this wasn´t the case for me.

One of the things that I did find was a very hard and cold winter. My family didn´t have money to buy the necessary clothing to protect ourselves from the low temperatures of New York, so many times we got cold—really, really cold. And when this cold chills your bones and stomach, it is difficult to think straight, especially in a land that is not your own, with a language that is totally foreign from your native tongue. Many of us immigrants sustain hardships that only we can understand, and we are usually misjudged and unfairly criticized.

Shame, fear, and depression were thus still present in my life. Without knowing a word of English, I felt stupid and limited—unable to express my ideas and my feelings. Nevertheless, I started to study and work at McDonald´s to help my family. I worked until almost midnight and then woke up early the next day to go to school. During the day, I was always looking for help from my teachers or the school counselor. At that time,

I was a fifteen-year-old kid, without any male or female friends. Young people my age used to make fun of me because I was different, given that I didn't speak the language and couldn't dress like the other girls because I didn't have the money to buy fashionable clothes; in my family, we got clothes from places where they sold them by the pound. Also, I couldn't hang out with other teenagers because I had to go to work after school. This caused me to be selective with my friendships. I didn't want to experiment with drugs, alcohol, or casual sex. I was shy and private about my things, and even though life was full of difficulties, the motivation that I had to help others and the faith that I had in finding a path to do it were always present in my mind and heart.

I remember that I used to arrive at school far earlier than anybody else in order to seek the help of teachers in the subjects that were harder for me and to be able to have a big breakfast. This early arrival also allowed me to sit in the front of everybody because I didn't see very well from the back. One time when I arrived late and all of the front row seats were taken, the teacher saw me squint to see the blackboard better and sent me to the nurse, who prescribed eyeglasses. This was a surprise because I didn't have the slightest clue that my sight was deficient; medical checkups were non-existent in my family. The eyeglasses, which were predictably unfashionable, made me look even weirder and prone to mockery, but for the first time in who knows how many years, I also saw everything with clarity… I quite possibly had perfect vision for the first time in seventeen years. So, I learned that symbolically, eyeglasses, like any tool, can miraculously improve your life. Nowadays I also understand that sometimes we need eyeglasses for the soul to help us see our path more clearly, and I offer them to you here in this book.

Back then, I felt like I had no time to waste because every minute opened a door to self improvement. I took every chance that I had to ask for advice from my teachers or the school counselor. I had the strong desire to go to college, but I didn't know which steps to take to be able to accomplish this goal. My mother also didn't have any idea of how to help me with this, and we didn't even have the money to pay for my education. My job didn't leave me time to practice any sport, and the only option that I had to earn a scholarship was by getting perfect grades. My school counselor, recognizing my efforts, supported me and helped me to maintain high grades while inspiring me to seize positive opportunities. She taught me to understand that effort, combined with consistency and good will, is always awarded. Even before I learned to trust myself, she always trusted me. That's why it's important to express to children and teenagers that we believe in them, in their abilities and best qualities, and to stimulate them to find new perspectives from which to look at life. When the school year was over, I registered for summer school because I wanted to finish secondary school fast, and I dreamt of starting college. Even if sometimes I felt that the world was crashing down, I had the necessary discipline, dedication, and drive to meet my goals. That was enough. I drew strength from the conviction that the only result of not working hard was being a prisoner of this same life that had offered me so little. I happily graduated from secondary school and registered at the State University of New York, New Paltz, where I got a degree in psychology, becoming the first person in my mother´s family with a college degree.

In college, I met the person who would later become my husband, the father of my two daughters, and my life partner. At that time, he aspired to become a producer or a representative of actors and wanted to continue his studies in Los Angeles. So, after his graduation we moved. He got accepted into Pepperdine University, and I got into UCLA, where I graduated with a masters degree in social work. It was a joy that my mother, sister, and brothers were present at the ceremony. I was finally reaping the fruits of my labor after so much struggle. Before long I was employed as a psychiatric social worker for the Family Preservation program of the Kedren Psychiatric Hospital and Mental Health Center in Los Angeles. I witnessed many cases of very sad psychological conditions, and I got to see how depression and the ailments of the mind and emotions can ruin lives and families. I felt that even if I worked 24 hours per day, I still would never be able to relieve and heal so much need. I felt so sad recognizing that in our current system of social wellbeing, there were no essential tools to give patients with mental illness solid treatment; instead, they saw themselves trapped in a cycle of therapy that keeps them dependent on it for several years without permanent improvement. It is a flaw of the system that I hope someday will be fixed. I understand that in some extreme cases complete recovery is impossible, but my own experience of personal healing leads me to believe that with the appropriate therapies, applied not only to the physical body but to the mind and spirit of the sick person, the radical healing of the disease is not only feasible but also doable.

Eventually, my husband and I returned to New York, where our daughters were born, but later, in 2003, we moved to Los Angeles again because my husband got offered a good job there. In time my economic situation stabilized; gradually, the poor girl who shared a bedroom with six relatives and a single bathroom with twenty people found herself living in a house full of rooms, including six bathrooms, in the prestigious and globally admired city of Beverly Hills. The ugly, ignorant, and deprived girl evolved into a beautiful and successful woman, dressed in the latest trends and swimming in abundance. Like in the story of Cinderella, my husband, a very handsome prince, cared for me and met my deep need for love. My daughters showered me with love and kisses where once I had only received beatings and abuse. The beauty, love, abundance, elegance, and respect started to fill the void of my shortcomings. My hunger for culture was also filled with my trips abroad to India, China, Turkey, France, Czechoslovakia, Venezuela, Saudi Arabia, Brazil, Japan, Qatar, Israel, Jordan, Spain, the Caribbean, Greece, Sweden, Russia, Italy, Morocco, China, and the list goes on... I encountered and experimented with things that I never would've imagined existed and that opened my mind and my social and cultural understanding. However, these blessings had a price that I wasn't emotionally prepared to pay.

My husband's job consumed all of his time, and we saw each other less and less. Despite having a wonderful man and spectacular father by my side—one who made sure his family wanted for nothing, which was new for me— I spent a lot of time alone with our two little girls. Loneliness, sadness, and unhealthy habits like a diet based on junk food and lack of proper rest, combined with the memory of a painful past, led me to a deep depression followed by a weakening and progressive disease. I suddenly found myself living a very dark phase, filled with fears and uncertainty, to the point that at times, I felt that I would seriously falter.

My husband´s and my families were far away, and I didn't yet have many friends. Every day I woke up with a sick body, but I still had to fulfill my obligations at home and at work. The reality is that sometimes we still aren't ready for happiness and wellbeing, even if the circumstances improve, because we just don't feel worthy, and we live with fear of that prison of sadness that chases us from our past. I think that once my life improved and my present circumstances were beautiful, I started to cry the sorrows of my past that I had worked so hard to hide. I felt so desperate that I think that this was the first time that I unleashed my symptoms and allowed depression to take over. There were days when I wanted to die because I was already tired of doctors and exams and had no strength left, but the fear of leaving my daughters without a mother pushed me to keep going. Everything was fine in my present except me, because of my past. Amongst other ailments, the disease that I developed, which is known as neutropenia, affected my blood. It is a severe hematological disorder with the potential of becoming lethal, and it affects the production of a certain type of white cell, called neutrophils, which oversee our bodies' primary defense against infections. It was hard for me to believe that I had developed such a dangerous disease, but so it was. I look back on that time as one of the hardest lessons that life has given me. I spent many hours visiting doctors in search of a solution and the medicines that would relieve the different ailments that plagued me as a result of my disease. At the same time, the medicines had a variety of side effects, and I lived fearing death with the next infection or the next fever. For the first time in my life, the idea that I was not going to survive frequently taunted me. I tried every means of hiding my fears and physical discomfort because I didn't want my daughters to see me so deteriorated, nor did I want the parents of the rest of the boys and girls at school to prohibit their children from playing with mine for fear of infection. Once again, I was scared and suffering in silence.

I needed medicine for everything. I remember one day, I started crying uncontrollably because I realized that I was taking 34 different types of medication. My marriage was also endangered, given that it was almost impossible for me to be alone with the girls while my husband worked abroad all the time. It was also challenging for him, as leaving his work would have signified an important setback in his career and personal life. Besides, at that time, my husband´s job was the only source of income for our family, since I had been forced to quit my job due to my weakness and my highly jeopardized immune system. But as the saying goes, "Everything in life happens for a reason." This experience was the best thing that could've happened because even if I didn't sense it at the time, my disease would become the path that would lead me to find the new Luz that I am now.

Healing is an internal, often times lonely, misunderstood, and judged path. It is something that we all face at some point in our lives. Even if we don't have severe diseases, we all have something to heal, whether it be of a physical, mental, or emotional nature. We only have to make the decision in our hearts and then undertake the unknown and extraordinary path towards our inner selves. It is there where we will find the key necessary to access the intuition that will lead us to the right cures and return us to our desired wellbeing. It is our right as human beings to live healthy, prosperous, happy lives. However, in most cases, we must make radical changes to achieve this. That was precisely my case.

Right when I didn't know what else to do and my head couldn't think of anything anymore, I decided not to remain silent any longer and to instead spoke to a friend who suggested that I make an appointment with a holistic healer. Having always chosen the traditional path of medicine, my first change was the acceptance of an alternative cure for my disease. Following the advice of my healer, I started my path towards recovery by changing my diet. Gradually, my food intake shifted to less-processed nutrition— food that was more natural and closer to Mother Earth. I started visiting local farmers' markets and choosing products grown without pesticides. I learned to read food labels and discovered which ingredients were healthy and which were harmful. I came to understand deep within me that having good health is the most important thing in life. With patience and love, we help ourselves to grow in the same way that we help our children to grow. Step by step, I followed the advice that I would've given to my patients, and in doing so I opened my mind to all kinds of physical and spiritual healing options. By changing my diet, I found that my depression and sadness were also changing, for what we eat directly affects our emotions and thoughts. Indeed, pre-made food, or fast food prepared with bad energy, eventually creates toxins in our bodies that finally end up making it sick.

With these changes, I slowly started to feel better, stronger. Not only did I start to heal physically but also mentally and emotionally by accepting my past just as it was, forgiving and forgetting the ones who had hurt me, pulling away from everything that caused me pain, and taking better care of myself. My doctors were skeptical of the cause of the change that was clearly visible in my follow-up exams, but I continued my efforts. In addition, when I was sufficiently recovered to begin making physical effort, I started working out. This also significantly helped me emotionally, physically, and mentally. My mind relaxed, easing the emotions, while my body burned toxins and grew stronger each time. I never thought that a poor diet could affect a human being so much. I never thought, up until this period, that nutrition was so important for the enjoyment of a life without pain or sickness. My own transformation is the reason why I decided to go back to school to study holistic medicine and nutrition at the Institute of Integrative Nutrition. Finally, after such a long path and after so many adventures and misadventures in life, I found my passion and my purpose. The desire that I always had in my heart to help people took shape within me, and I finally found the way that I could best serve my neighbor: by becoming a guide and counselor for their physical, emotional, mental, and spiritual healing. Having suffered for many years and emerging safe and sound from it, I now feel deep empathy for another person´s pain and sorrow.

I know how hard the path to one's own healing can be,

but I also have absolute certainty that it can be done. One can free him or herself from sickness and regain perfect health if he or she addresses it with faith, determination, and consistency. It is a very personal and inner choice—one that I know well. I am now completely healthy, filled with enthusiasm and the joy of living, and I lead a life surrounded by love and beauty. I acknowledge my past as my best teacher—a teacher that has provided me with the necessary lessons that helped me to get to this wonderful gift that is my present. Thanks to all that has happened to me thus far, I became a better mother, wife, and professional. Even though I recognize that life tests us many times and is filled with challenges and problems, I can finally say that I feel like a complete human being.

I would like to close this chapter recalling one of the stories of Mara and Buddha: Mara was an evil demon who was jealous of Buddha's discipline and determination. The legend goes that Mara ordered his army to attack Buddha, who was meditating under a tree where he later found enlightenment. Mara´s soldiers shot hundreds of arrows in order to annihilate Buddha, but as the arrows got close to Buddha, they became nothing but flowers that fell to his feet.

This is a possibility that is available to everyone: we can turn the difficulties that we encounter in life into opportunities that fall at our feet. It seems like a fantasy, I know; I found it hard to believe in such a thing myself, but after having learned from my own experience and witnessed how other people have also done it, I can claim with absolute certainty that you can also achieve it, if you put your mind in it.

As Hippocrates said, "The natural healing force within each of us is the greatest force in getting well."

CHAPTER 2

Breaking the chains!

I have felt in my own flesh the feeling of being trapped and at a dead end, thinking and feeling that everything is going to go the wrong way— that the world isn't a safe place for me and that the only thing that I can expect from the future is bigger calamities. I know the overwhelming anxiety that those limiting thoughts and feelings can create, and I understand the process that leads a person to restrict him or herself mentally, emotionally, or physically because, as I illustrated earlier, I have lived it. I am not the only one, though. Those who have endured suffocating experiences or have met people who suffer, mostly in silence, while trapped in their own mental, physical, or emotional prisons know what I am talking about. The physical prison is the most obvious one and possibly the easiest to detect, as it mainly consists of diseases, impairments, and everything related to our material world. This type of prison can't be hidden for too long… neither from ourselves nor from others.

I have no doubt that my disease was a consequence of chronic depression, anxiety, and an unhealthy diet. In the past, I had worked very hard on my feelings, but despite this effort, it was bodily disease that showed me the final path towards my healing. To heal myself, I first needed to recognize that the necessary strength and drive to face such a big enterprise were within myself. So, I had to begin by accepting myself just as I was at that time, with all of my strengths and weaknesses. As a second step, I had to attend to my own needs and listen to myself so that I could follow my internal guide; in that way, I could start to detoxify not only my body but my mind and emotions as well. As soon as I made the firm decision to do it and started working on it, the symptoms that harassed me so frequently started to decrease and eventually disappeared.

I would like to share here some of the tools that helped me to heal myself. As a first measure, I started looking around me and counting my blessings. When you decide to change, destiny gives you the support to do so. My personal destiny has always been God. One day, as I was exploring the changes that I had to make in my life, I happened upon this prayer on the website secretosdelalma.com, and it had exactly the words that I wanted to express:

Healing Prayer

Heavenly Father. Thank you for my life in this new day and for your protection. Show me what I must learn from the health problems that I am facing. Show me the area of my life that needs to be transformed. By healing my soul, my body also heals. Help me forgive those who in some way have made me suffer. Show me when I have done harm to others, so I can feel your forgiveness. Thank you father. I request it, as Jesus taught me. Amen.

I must acknowledge that recognizing my blessings took some time, for the memories of my past kept getting in the way of my efforts. When you grow up in such a negative environment like I did – and I know that, unfortunately, many share this experience – it doesn't matter how nice your life is in the present, for the negative cloud that you have lived with for so many years continues to hang over you, and the thought that you don't deserve anything good, or that it is just a matter of time before everything goes wrong again, keeps torturing you.

Have you heard the expression "living in a golden cage"? In these cases, you are the cage. In my experience, when I tried to focus on the positive things in my life, my own family doomed me by making me feel bad in one way or another because I wanted to be different—because I wanted to break the cycle that had made us all miserable. I remembered that in a lecture that I attended at the Institute of Integrative Nutrition, one of the speakers mentioned that there were times when, in order to heal, it is necessary for the person to get away from his or her family, for there were cases in which it was the family, with their drama and negative energy, that could prevent the person from moving on. In the beginning, I was surprised to hear this, but I then understood that it wasn't about not loving my family or having to completely get away from them – even though there are times when getting away for some time is the right path – but I needed to remain aware of their behaviors and manipulations in order to avoid letting them sink me in their swamp.

It is worth mentioning that each healing effort is individual and personal, and that even if the members of a family have gone through the same events, each one of them deals with the experience in a different way. You may be part of a family that, like mine, is used to a routine based on repeating the same story over and over, but one day you decide that this is no longer for you, and you want to break free from those chains. It is a very common reality that your family won't understand you, that they are not ready to hear you say, "Enough of this! I want to be happy! I don't want to continue with this lifestyle!" In response, they treat you as the "black sheep," getting mad at you, mocking you, or distracting you with their own dramas and problems, thereby preventing you from rising up out of the swamp. It is in that precise moment when you must be aware and realize how your family or the ones closest to you can work either in favor or against your healing, and this is why recognizing the situation will become one of the most important tools for you.

Once I reflected on my family history, I started to thank them for the shared experiences and for all of the lessons that I received from them. Then I could start loving from a different place for the first time, without the drama. For example, when negative feelings towards my mother overtook me, like the resentment that was very much alive in me regarding her rejection, instead of punishing myself for what my heart and mind were experiencing, I first accepted that these emotions where momentarily a part of my life, and then I focused on the understanding and compassion that I needed to offer to my mother. In doing so, I began to understand that she had done her best with the tools and knowledge that she had. After all, she was also a victim of destiny and of the socio-economic and cultural environment in which she was raised. My mother never had a mother who offered her a caring upbringing and a respectable education. Rather, she grew up in an environment that was completely patriarchal, where women were treated as inferior beings and weren't respected as they deserved to be. Despite that reality, though, she managed to give her children a better life. Even without much education, she offered us all the chance to become college graduates, to have a life without drugs, alcohol, or violence, and to grow with the tools to reach wellbeing and economic security. In acknowledging this, I saw my resentment transform into admiration, respect, and compassion for her suffering and sacrifices. I put myself in her place, and I imagined the grief, pain, and difficulties that she endured while separating herself from her children for four years. How much she must have needed us! And then she had to help us get through every day without the help of a partner, all while overcoming a host of daily obstacles just to be able to keep going. I believe in my heart that she has always been my example and my inspiration.

I did the same work with my father, who was also very difficult for me to forgive. At times, it seemed impossible to achieve it, for the abuse had been extensive, and the wounds were so deep that I never got to completely clean them. I had a fervent desire to forgive, even if I didn't know how, so I clung to God and His help. In these moments of silence, I could see my father from another perspective, like a scared child, perhaps, who had been victim of the violence that he was so used to spreading himself. My anger gave way to a deep sadness when I put myself in this man´s place, and I understood that having lost an eye, he was hindered in his ability to support a family with four children. I felt the shame that he must have experienced in an environment where a man gained respect based on the kind of support and contribution that he offered his wife and kids. I grasped the pressured that he must have felt when encountering the accusing looks of other men. I don't know how I would have acted in a similar situation. From this place, I could understand him and forgive him, and, at the same time, I could forgive myself, thus leaving space to fulfill the healing of my body. I saw my father only once more after I left the Dominican Republic, and unfortunately it was at his funeral, as he died very young from a stroke. I would've liked to have given him one last hug and say to him that, despite it all, I loved him.

In this time of focusing on forgiveness, the words of Maya Angelou inspired me: "Forgiveness. It's one of the greatest gifts you can give yourself, to forgive. Forgive everybody. You are relieved of carrying that burden of resentment. You really are lighter. You feel lighter. You just drop that."

Gratitude for all that I had also became a fundamental

part of my routine. I used daily statements and took the time to sit down in silence and spend some moments with God, thanking Him for all of the good things and also for what I considered bad as well. I worked hard to focus on the positive instead of giving so much importance to the negative and the misery that comes with it. There were certainly days when I did better than others; however, I accepted my moments of frustration, and without punishing myself for what I felt, I continued on, centered in my work, taking baby steps each day. This is something that takes time, but once you are trained to understand, forgive, and thank, the change within you starts to flow. Even now, with all of the inner work that I have done, it is very difficult for me to speak of my childhood, but I keep repeating to myself again and again that everything that happened to me is not my fault. I was a victim of certain circumstances, but instead of remaining within this victim role, I focused on the power of healing— something that is inherent to each one of us— and I decided to ascend from the pit of victimization so that I wouldn't repeat the same history that I had learned in my family, a trend that is very common with people who have been abused. In this way, my daughters also benefitted, and future generations will benefit as well, because the prison sentence ended with me.

I also appreciate the disease that led me to the healing

of my mind and emotions, for emotional and mental limitations aren't that easy to recognize and are intimately connected to the ailments of the body. I wish for you with all my heart that you don't have to face disease to realize the changes that you need to make in order to be happy.

Many times, the ailments of the body can be avoided when you make yourself conscious of the negative thoughts and feelings that hide in the darkness of your being. Don't wait for your inner limitations to start manifesting in your external world before you recognize and heal them; identify them before they impact in your daily life. Learn the way that this perfect system works: I think, I feel, and I act. Remember that thoughts become realities for us, and these thoughts drive us to certain kind of feelings that then turn into actions. This works well if we have what we call "positive thoughts" that lead us to being happy and thankful, and which have consequences that benefit our physical and material world. But if the same thing that happened to me happens to you (when my thoughts turned against me and started attacking me), you will feel bad and will create all kinds of problems for yourself—some simpler and others harder to solve.

The most used sentence in my house was, "you are worthless." Unfortunately, I never had the joy of hearing, "good work!" or "that was really great!" The programming of the "you are worthless" sentiment, which was often reinforced by physical abuse, had become impressed upon me so deeply that it created fears, which were mainly unfounded. Even if I didn't realize it, though, these fears were filling me with low self-esteem and fear of failure while also frustrating many of my desires to do something new or even to try to move forward in life. Even if there were moments when I did overcome this crippling fear, I never expected a positive result. When you constantly hear that "you are worthless," especially from your parents and close relatives, you gradually start to believe it in such a way that one day you will find yourself trapped in a vicious circle that isn't easy to break free from. I have lived this cycle: even in moments when I had successfully achieved my goals, I kept hearing a taunting voice repeat, "you are worthless," which caused me to eventually sink into a state of depression and riddled me with the anxiety that my success could end at any moment. It whispered incessantly that I didn't have the ability to maintain my achievement or that my success had merely been a "coincidence" or a "stroke of luck," but never the result of my constant efforts. As a result of such thoughts, I couldn't enjoy anything.

The negative statements that we grow up with can

remain ever-present, ready to darken everything that is beautiful around us. What happens is that the thoughts may or may not be based in reality, but if the mind believes it, then it becomes as good as a real. The good news is that thoughts are not fixed; they aren't made of thick matter, even if they may often seem so. Thoughts are really made of fluctuating energy that can be re-directed and modified. In other words, thoughts can be changed before they have the time to create negative feelings that will create chaos in your material world. As Louise Hay so eloquently says, "I change my life when I change my thinking... And it is time for me to acknowledge that I create my own reality with my thoughts. If I want to change my reality, then it is time for me to change my mind."

Changing the way that I thought was a path that initially seemed impossible to follow, but with time and practice, this path revealed its many rewards. It's important to train your mind to see things from another perspective, and to know that you can do it. As I focused on the positive side and on appreciation, I could recognize that each one of my achievements, however small they might've been, was a step towards my freedom. I was ecstatic to stop repeating with my daughters the same mistakes that my parents had made while raising me. This was, indeed, a huge success. That I had a healthy relationship with my girls, with open communication and mutual trust, felt like a miracle. Step by step, I accepted that it wasn't necessary to keep carrying the restraining thoughts of my past, and this acceptance burrowed deeper and deeper within me, allowing me to move forward and to recognize that my current situation was different. The inspiring words of writer Doe Zantamata are relevant here: "Too often, we carry around those things from our past that hurt us the most. Don't let past pain rob you of your present happiness. You had to live through it in the past, and that cannot be changed, but if the only place it lives today is in your mind, then forgive, let go, and be free."

When you wake up, try thanking God for one more day of life, for your family and friends, for your health even if it isn't the ideal that you would like to have. Count your blessings even if you think they are few. Thank God for the bed that you woke up in, the water with which you´re going to brush your teeth, your teeth themselves. There are people who have neither a bed, nor water, nor teeth. There are human beings who are facing much worse situations than you, who live in areas destroyed by war, where they never know when a bomb is going to fall on them. There are those who live in total poverty, who have nothing to call their own, whose existence is riddled with garbage—both literal and metaphorical.

I remember a trip to India that opened my eyes to a reality of overwhelming scarcity, worse than I had endured in La Romana. One thing that impacted me significantly was when I set foot outside of the Mumbai airport and could see children, women, and elderly people throwing themselves at our taxi while begging for food. In India, I also saw bodily deformities that I never imagined existed. Locals later explained to me that many families deliberately deform their own children so that people feel sorry for them when they beg. These children endured acid burns, mutilations, cuts, and other horrors at the hands of their own family members. I felt deep pain and inadequacy witnessing so much suffering, and I appreciated the blessings that I had so much more as a result.

While I healed and expressed gratitude every day, the feelings of depression, low self esteem, and victimization decreased incrementally until one day they became inaudible. Even so, there are times when they still visit me, but with much less power than in the past. When they do, I thank them for being a part of my experience in this life. I also talk to them, immediately letting them know that their visit is only temporary. I know that, as the owner of my own mind, I have control over my feelings, and I can choose not to keep feeding them. It's like when you have visitors in your home: you know that they aren't going to stay forever.

The same is true of thoughts.

Another tool that has also continuously helped me is to focus on an activity that I enjoy. I try to engage in something enjoyable daily, or as often as I possibly can. For example, I have always loved music, and it has the power to make me feel instantly better, especially music with motivating lyrics, but also those song with sad lyrics that drive me to get my emotions out instead of keeping them bottled inside.

As Elton John says, "Music has healing power. It has the ability to take people out of themselves for a few hours." As I listen to my favorite songs, I feel like I can freely let go of all of the toxic feelings and sensations; I can toss them out and cut them off. I have a routine of taking a 45-minute daily walk, where I focus on gratitude and meditation. While I do so, I listen to music.

Some of my favorite songs are:"Step by Step" by Whitney Houston, "What a Wonderful World" by Louis Armstrong, "Whatever Will Be, Will Be" by Doris Day, "Get up Stand Up" by Bob Marley, "Imagine" by John Lennon, "Flashdance...What a Feeling" by Irene Cara, " I Can See Clearly Now" by Johnny Nash and "Let It Go" by Idina Menzel. I think you might notice a theme in my song choices, don't you?

While I used these tools of self-improvement, I also started to change my diet more, integrating additional nutritious foods and less fast or artificial food, all of which I complemented with regular physical exercise. The more relaxation and peace that I found in my mind, the bigger and deeper the positive changes that manifested themselves in my body. As you probably know, the connection between mind and body has been demonstrated in several studies; you can´t fix one part without a corresponding improvement in the other— they go hand-in-hand. That is why good doctors ask their patients about their mental and emotional health— because it directly affects the patient's wellbeing or distress. In the following chapters, I will address this fundamental union in more detail—a union that we often times ignore. With this same principle of mind/body union, I will begin explaining to you the prisons that we find ourselves in during our healing process.

"Only when the mind is free of ideas and beliefs can it act correctly."

– Jiddu Krishnamurti.

Mental Prison

You are only a victim if you let yourself be…

For those of us who have been raised with challenges or exposed to various traumas, it is common to create negative ideas, beliefs, and thoughts that lead us to an existence plagued by unhappiness. While my thought process may be very different from that of someone who has gone through an experience similar mine, there are characteristics that we share, like deeply rooted negative thoughts and ideas in our conscious and subconscious mind, which will inevitably attract the external manifestation of those calamities that we so want to avoid. If you have a thought that says, for example, "nobody loves me," it is very possible that you feel alone and abandoned, and this can translate into the use of toxic substances like drugs, alcohol, sugar, or food to fill the void caused by a lack of love. Or you could be surrounding yourself with people who mistreat and reject you, thereby reinforcing the belief that "nobody loves me." As I have illustrated, I have also gone through similar experiences with members of my family, so I understand you and encourage you to deviate from that, as I know in my heart that you can do it. My pattern of feeling that "I am worthless" often prevented me from accepting positive comments about myself. Even when people said them, I often didn't hear them. I only heard blame and insecurity, which empowered the self-loathing beliefs that, "what you were told is not true.

You should be ashamed. You are forcing people to say nice things about you because of your attitude of self-pity." My mind would taunt me with falsities like, "they are lying out of obligation. You know that you´re a loser," or "don't listen to them. They say that to everybody just to look good. They can see perfectly well that you are worthless." Demeaning internal comments such as these kept lambasting me until I was so mad at myself that I punished myself with physical ailments, unpleasant emotional experiences, sugar and fast food, and the inability to establish a serious significant relationship with someone else, whether out of love, friendship, or business. I alienated myself from people, immersing myself in my loneliness. I remember so many times when I was in a group and was feeling scared of even opening my mouth and saying something "not worth hearing." Such an attitude leads you to isolation and keeps you from socializing, which is so necessary for personal and professional progress. Some typical example of limiting thoughts that plague so many of us are:

- I am worthless.

- Everything turns out wrong for me. These goals and dreams are not for me, so what good does it do to even try?

- I can't do it. I'm incapable of doing anything right.

- I´m not good enough for anything.

- This would be a better world if I didn´t exist.

- Everything is going to turn out wrong as it always has.

- My life has no meaning. Nothing is worth it.

- Everything is going to turn out wrong, so why make an effort or fight for something. It's not going to work anyway.

- Whatever I do, I can't take the reins of my life, and I will never be able to.

- Nobody cares about me. Nobody loves me. I have no value to anyone.

- I am a victim of the circumstances that surround me. My family, friends, society, etc., are to blame for what happens to me.

- This time I got it right by coincidence. It's not going to repeat itself. I better quit before I fail.

- I am right to think this way. What I think is the truth.

- I don't care about anybody because nobody cares about me.

- Everybody judges and criticizes me. It is better to go unnoticed –nobody sees or hears me.

- My life goes from bad to worse, and it´s not going to improve.

- In this life there is no salvation. We have come to suffer.

The list is endless because once we give free rein to our thoughts, they procreate and start dragging you into an abyss from which it's very difficult to escape. But, as I mentioned earlier, the good news is that this can be used to our advantage because thoughts can be transformed into our allies. In my personal consultations, my clients sometimes tell me that they find it impossible to think differently— that they are the victims of their own minds and that even if they try, they can´t modify the course of their beliefs. It is possible that certain socially ingrained or inherited ideas are so imbedded within us that we can´t even imagine who we would be without them. It is very sad that in some cultures, like in the one that I was raised in, it is common for women to suffer low self-esteem and, in extreme cases, to let themselves be beaten and abused. This is a consequence of the superior importance that men have, for they are considered more intelligent and capable in every way over their female partners.

There are innumerable cases of mothers who are charged with "doing nothing" when they choose to stay at home and raise the kids. Many husbands come home in the afternoon and ask them each day, "What have you done today? I have worked like a dog all day to bring you money, and you are here at home like a bum, doing nothing!" Doing nothing? Is that what cleaning the house, having food prepared, taking care of the education and wellbeing of the kids, assisting with school homework, attending meetings with teachers, taking care of the family when they get sick means? Does all of that account for nothing? Housewives are mothers, servants, cooks, psychologists, drivers, nurses, cleaners, mediators, secretaries, personal assistants, and so much more. And they do it all in service of the family. It is very wrong that they feel guilty of "doing nothing."

The same negativity happens with racial, religious, and

socio-economical discrimination. It leaves very deep scars and feelings of inferiority, even when the generation that has been the victim of such discrimination is not our own, but rather our parents' or grandparents' generation. There was a time when I filled my head with questions like, "why is this happening to me? Why me? What have I done wrong to deserve this?" And the corresponding answer was, "because I don't deserve better. Because I'm not good enough," and "because it´s not enough that I try. I'm no good at anything anyway." The truth is, even with these ideas flooding my head, I still wanted to improve myself and be happy, just like you do. Through daily gratitude, I slowly started changing my inner dialogue. Instead of asking myself, "why me?" I said, "why not?" I wondered, "what should I learn from this experience? What has this situation come to teach me?" I didn't try to find immediate answers, though. I was mostly exploring the questions, and I let everything else come on its own. After all, from an unfavorable situation, wonderful events can arise. I often thank God for my ability to help families and kids in need and have been abused, as I can understand them very well thanks to the situation that I grew up in. This shows me that there are times when losses bring us enormous benefits.

I understand that there are times when it seems difficult, and maybe even alarming, to let go of certain kind of thoughts that have been with us for years. The uncertainty of not knowing what we are going to put in their place can cause us fear and uncertainty. This is the case for so many women who have been abused by their husbands, either physically, emotionally, or both. They often have a hard time leaving their partners and the thoughts and feelings related to them. It's not that they enjoy been beaten or threatened, but for very individual and particular reasons, they simply stay in a negative relationship. They may fear that they will never find nor deserve a better man, or they may feel insecure about how they are going to sustain themselves financially if they are on their own. They may fear for their children, or fear some kind of familial or religious pressure. Whatever the reason, they remain in their relationship, battling an impossible situation. Ultimately, though, we all seek wellbeing, and even if we don't realize it, we are growing and developing all the time.

As the human being evolves, so do his or her thoughts. We feel the need to detoxify our minds from the ideas and judgments that are no longer useful to us and that, on the contrary, hinder us. Everything around us screams, "It´s time for a change! The time has come to align with yourself, with the person you really are. Leave the old behind. Start moving towards the new!" The fact that you are reading this book means that you are ready to begin your path towards healing and to reclaim your inherent wellbeing. Your mind is opening to new ideas, so let them in with hope and faith that the answer that you´ve been looking for is in your hand here and now.

"You don't have to control your thoughts; just stop letting them control you." – Dan Millman

Emotional Prison

If we keep on giving life to the wrong thoughts and ideas mentioned above, sooner or later they will create a habit in our way of feeling. The fear and insecurity that I know so intimately are usually found in people who have been victims of physical and verbal violence in their early childhood and in the years that follow. It feels as if the whole world is against you, and a constant fear invades everything that you do and every step that you take.

During one of the sessions that I had with my holistic healer, as we were working on my fears, he advised me to close my eyes for a few moments and imagine that I had parents or relatives who loved, protected, and nourished me. He asked me to focus on seeing the hands of my mother and my father caressing me with love while they told me how intelligent and beautiful I was. My healer helped me to imagine the encouraging words coming out of my parents' mouths and to receive with gratitude the tools that they offered me to develop successfully in life. For a moment I felt safe, knowing that nothing bad was going to happen to me because I had the care and support of my family that was always there for me. I felt so incredibly good. When the session ended, I went home and kept thinking about how beautiful it must be for those people who have grown up loving, respecting, and appreciating the joys of family—those who have had company and support in the difficult moments of life and who were honored in each achievement, no matter how small. I thought of the people whom I know with those characteristics. They did things because they felt them, without being afraid of what other people would say, as they trusted themselves and their own abilities. An athlete and champion, Jennifer Bricker, came to mind. Having been born without legs, she was abandoned in the hospital by her parents the day she was born. She was fortunate though, as her adoptive parents taught her that there were no limits to anything that she wanted to achieve. They told her that the only thing that was forbidden was saying "I can´t." So, Jennifer grew up believing in herself and became a champion tumbler and successful acrobat and aerialist. In addition to her professional success, the absence of

"I can't" allowed her to investigate her biological family, and she eventually learned that Dominique Moceanu, a gold medalist in gymnastics and her childhood idol, was her biological sister! Jennifer is a wonderful example of the miracles that can come true if you believe in yourself.

On the contrary, people who are emotionally trapped are mainly insecure, feel lonely, don't believe in themselves, and mostly have no idea of what their abilities and virtues are. Instead of "moving forward," they "go in circles" and can't progress in their lives. They are overwhelmed by fears of all kinds and suffer from depression, anxiety, resentment, and emotional dependency, among other things. They live in a self-imposed prison and feel incapable of getting out of the labyrinth that they are trapped in. I know that it isn't easy to stay away from this abyss, but I tell you from the bottom of my heart that it can be done. The secret is recognizing the feelings that disturb us, listening to what they are telling us, and working with them to eliminate them. The truth is that the sooner that we recognize the problem, the faster we can work on the solution, because where there is a problem, there is also a solution.

It´s possible that in certain stages, the pains are so big and deep that you may need professional help to work through the emotions that they cause you. Personally, I keep thanking the universe because it provided me with the counselor at my New York high school. I will never tire of thanking that woman for giving me the opportunity to express myself emotionally, without feeling ashamed, guilty, weak, or stupid. She was always willing to listen and help me see my setbacks from another point of view. It was with my counselor that I learned to accept the feelings that affected me as a part of myself, and to be able to work with them and move on. With absolute patience and real interest in my wellness, she guided me towards the best decisions for my education and my progress.

Even when you find professional help, you might believe that you will never be able feel free to express yourself emotionally. I know— it wasn't easy for me either. In my home, these things were forbidden and punished with a blow and a "shut up! You don't know what you´re saying" or "you´re an ungrateful girl, and life will punish you for being so ungrateful." It took a lot of effort to allow myself to recognize and express my feelings. I had to start by loving myself, taking care of my body, improving my self-esteem, and appreciating my achievements and successes, even if they were only small seeds. I had the desire to learn to say "no" to the situations and people who caused me discomfort, and I had to learn not to feel guilty for doing so. It was gradual work that has been increasing and deepening with the passing of the years. I equate it to climbing a spiral ladder, and of ding fruits of the seeds that I had planted while I ascended it. When I could start expressing my emotions, I understood that for so long I had hosted the belief that my feelings weren't important to anyone, and that I hadn't given them any importance. How wrong I was! Expressing my emotions offered me liberation, and I think that it even changed my way of breathing, which was now far more relaxed and calm. I repeat: change begins with learning to take care of yourself. That's why, when I work with families, I focus on reminding the mothers that they have to look after themselves—pamper, take care of themselves, and express their emotions and needs—because if they get sick or sad and become unsatisfied, their children and husbands will suffer as well. I mention mothers because they are usually the ones who forget about themselves as they look after the other members of the family, but this advice also goes for fathers.

In short, emotions are an essential part of the human experience. They work like radar showing us where we are on our life paths, and it isn't good to ignore them, whether they are positive or negative emotions. For example, fear can actually be positive when it warns us, "don't do this. It's going to harm you." Likewise, crying and sadness can tell us, "enough of this situation. You have to change it or you´re going to get sick!" Frustration drives us to seek new goals; pain opens our heart to comprehension and compassion; happiness lets us know that we are on the right path for our mission in life; love lets us take care of one another; enthusiasm leads to victory… Can you start to understand the importance of not repressing this emotional radar? When you repress it, you lose yourself. Is like throwing the map of your destiny out the window of your car. You will never get to the right place if you do so! Your emotions can become a useful guide for you as long as you use them for progress.

"The way you feel is your indicator to know if you are in synchrony with who you've become or not. When you feel excited, when you feel APPRECIATION, when you feel that enthusiasm towards life, you are moving in the direction of who you really are." – Abraham Hicks

Physical Prison

This is the third and last prison that I'm going to discuss with you. As I previously expressed, I learned from personal experience that our bodies, emotions, and minds are firmly connected. Once I was trapped in this cycle of unhealthy emotions and thoughts, my physical body was, consequently, affected. Beyond the sickness or discomfort that you may experience, there are also unhealthy behaviors that we frequently acquire while thinking that they are going to relieve our mental and emotional pains. Alcohol, drugs, food, violence, casual sex, abuse of all types, and isolation even can cause temporary satisfaction, but, in the long run, they exacerbate the initial problem, dragging the person into a deep abyss. The reality is that if these behaviors worked, the loneliness, desperation, depression, violence and suicide rates would go down instead of up. In my case, and in the case of other people who have successfully abandoned harmful behaviors and found the liberating key to overcoming painful difficulties in the past, it was essential to call upon the courage and bravery that we all have inside of us. I know you can do it too. During my inner work, I found myself once and again succumbing to the habit of not knowing how to take care of myself, which is almost inevitable when you grow up in a home lacking love and nurturing. You don't know that you have the option of loving and protecting yourself, and when you try, it is possible that you even feel guilty for not serving others who "surely deserve it more than you do." It is good to help others, and we all have that inherent instinct, but if you are not ok, how do you expect to help other people? Abraham Hicks refers to the right way of helping in one of his speeches: "It is a wonderful thing to help others, but you must do it from your position of strength and alignment."

Try thinking a little more of yourself and your needs; learn to accept help when it is offered, and you will see that the unpleasant physical manifestations will gradually start shifting towards improvement. Especially if you experience physical pain, you will recognize the difference right away because it will probably decrease considerably. Migraines and other kinds of headaches, for example, can be avoided if you look after yourself as soon as you feel the first symptoms. When you start to engage in self-respect and self-care, those extra pounds that you've been carrying might also disappear, mainly because you start putting in your mouth only those things that are healthy for your body—you treat it well, and you don't want to harm it because you love it.

While I wasn't taking care of my body and my feelings, my immune system was compromised, leading to my disease, which acted as a demand for a return to balance in my life. Stress was my number-one enemy, and I know that it is for many people. In our contemporary society, we may feel that it is expected that we live in a state of heightened stress, and this state is so common that we don't even pay attention to it anymore, but our bodies do. Stress can lead to weight gain, cardiac and respiratory diseases, blood pressure fluctuations, digestive diseases like ulcers and stomach aches, sexual impotence and loss of libido, among other ailments. Indeed, stress is one of the main enemies of our health and wellbeing.

Stress provides a typical example of how the mixture of our emotional and mental prisons affect us, since stress is first born in the mind because of a reaction to a particular kind of external pressure, and it is then translated into our physical/emotional processes as excessive fatigue, overeating, irritability, worriedness, and tension, among other debilitating conditions. Always remember that the key to our recovery is in our pockets, and imprisonment is completely self-imposed, even if this seems terribly difficult to believe. You may be wondering, "how would I chose this disease or this loss if what I want is just the opposite?" I thought this frequently, but with work I learned that, truly, it is not what we choose but what we create, mainly through our unconscious thoughts, feelings, and actions. I didn't realize that I followed a certain pattern of thoughts and conduct because this pattern was so imbedded within me that it manifested itself naturally, until I learned that what is actually natural is leading a happy, calm, and healthy life. I, like many people, had forgotten that.

Next time you're conscious of repeating a bad habit, try

to remember that the decisions that we make in the present affect our future, and they can hold us captive for life or free us forever, thus allowing us to finally find light, happiness, and success in abundance. In my personal consultancy, I have come across different cases of people who are trapped in a self-imposed jail. Initially, I listen to them patiently and with empathy in order to then develop a working plan that helps them to free themselves from past traumas. One of the most important parts of our plan is developing objectives and goals together, so that the client has a clear direction on which to focus. In doing so, my clients immediately start to become conscious that the success of our program depends only on themselves. My work as a counselor is to help them recognize how their emotions affect them. Once we have identified their prisons and are confident that they are aware of them, I guide them towards a victory. This sometimes happens quickly and sometimes a bit slower, but I am always certain that they can overcome the obstacles that prevent them from developing their maximum power as human beings so that they reach their goals.

Each process is a unique, personal, and wonderful workshop because my clients always learn to find their own tools instead of sinking into a codependent relationship with me, which can often happen between a patient and a therapist. I would like to mention here that I have personally always avoided co-dependent relationships where a person attends therapeutic appointments for years without truly going anywhere. Unfortunately, in many first world countries, this type of cycle happens often because doctors and patients see themselves wrapped in an economic entanglement where if the latter is cured, then the financial benefit for the physician dries up; the money spent on therapy and the expensive medications that go along with it stops flowing. I witnessed this when I worked as a social worker and family therapist for the state, and this cycle was one of the reasons, along with the change that my disease provoked, that I ultimately decided to open my private practice where transparency is fundamental.

"A positive attitude causes a chain reaction of positive thoughts, events and outcomes. It is a catalyst and it sparks extraordinary results." – Wade Boggs

CHAPTER 3

Prisoners and liberated, from celebrities to people just like you

We've already seen the way in which our prisons, invented or inherited, become obstacles to the realization of our purpose in life, and how they prevent us from achieving the happiness and mental peace that we chase daily. In Annex 1 of this book, you will find situations that are likely very similar to what you are living. The cases that I present happened to people just like you and like me—people who one day arrived at my consultation with a problem that was often a reflection or a consequence of living in this prison that I have told you so much about. I recommend you read their stories so that you better understand how to locate the key that opens the door of that prison and lets you leave behind that dark, humid, and narrow space that has been a barrier to defining and fulfilling your life's work.

These types of cases don't only happen in my private consultation, however. They have also affected many people who, despite blessings like fame, talent, and fortune, weren't able to escape the confinement of that prison of their past. As a result, they abandoned this world, leaving behind the perplexity and sadness of those who admired and loved them. In Annex 2, I would like to share some such cases, not only because have they inspired me throughout my life and my search, but also because they have been useful as a lesson for my own progress; like so many others, I used to think that cases of abuse and serious family issues only existed among people of low economic, social, or cultural circumstances, but that is not the case.

Despite their international recognition and success, Whitney Houston, Michael Jackson, and Robin Williams all lived locked up inside of personal prisons. I know that many times we think that there are people, like them, who have it all. There were certainly times when I even found myself criticizing wealthy people, or people who had had a better education than me, because I naively believed that they could never understand me or feel any empathy for my situation, or for other people´s suffering. I also used to feel a lot of outrage for not having had the same joy as other people who were surely "much happier than me." These feeling came to the surface more frequently when I moved to Beverly Hills. I couldn't find anything in common with the people who lived there, and despite the fact that I communicated with them and listened to their experiences and life histories, I felt a vast chasm between us. For example, there were women who complained of being bored because they had no jobs, nor the need to have them, or others were unhappy because their husbands where never present and didn't pay them much attention as a result of their demanding careers. These women possessed significance material abundance, and their family didn't experience scarcity of any kind.

From my point of view, these problems seemed very small compared to those of the abused girls and homeless mothers who didn't know how they were going to support their children or where the next meal was going to come from, not to mention other sorrowful cases that I dealt with each day at work. When I got sick, however, I learned not to judge others' problems for the size of what they "appeared to be" because, at the end of the day, they are all setbacks that compromise our quality of life, to a greater or lesser extent. Each person knows his or her problems and the level of stress that these cause them. What for some may seem foolish for others might mean the world. I could prove this in the moments when I had it all—a family that loved me, a job I enjoyed, money— and yet

I felt like the unhappiest human on earth: sad, sick, and without an escape in sight. Now I know that if you don´t feel good about yourself, what you have isn't worth much. I also understand that the prisons that I talked about before can affect anyone, no matter their skin color, social status, image, beauty, financial status, or professional success.

Unfortunately, many "prisoners" stayed on the confined path, fell into deep unhappiness, and could no longer pull themselves back out, so they sheltered themselves in addictions, or misfortune, or, in some extreme cases, even death. Thank God, many others could overcome their challenges and get out of the prison that they were in. I will call them the "liberated." This was the case with Oprah Winfrey, César Chávez, and Bethany Hamilton, the surfer girl who lost an arm after a shark attack and, thanks to her tenacity and faith, provided my daughters and me with a very strong role model. These and other such examples can be found in Annex 3.

I hope that the cases that I present in the annexes, the "prisoners" as much as the "liberated," provide you with inspiration and enthusiasm to change those things that are blocking you from seeing the beauty and wellbeing that surround you. I would like to make clear that I never have the intention of comparing or judging anyone, for I consider each life a miracle, no matter what happens in it. The experiences of everyone mentioned above have helped me to overcome my own problems and challenges. They have helped me to understand that we can all go through adverse situations, no matter what their origin is, and we can choose to free ourselves or to sink. The answer to this dilemma lies solely within ourselves.

In anticipation of one of the characters mentioned in Annex 3, I'd like to tell you more about one of my consistent sources of inspirations: Oprah. The fact that she was born in such poverty and that she was raped many times as a child has had a great impact on me. In my personal and therapeutic experience, I have had many patients who grew up in similar conditions, and it is very difficult for people who were sexually abused in their childhoods to stop reliving that abuse in their heads and, in some way, in their lives, whether that means by developing a debilitating disease or continuing on as victim of the same type of circumstances. However, Oprah managed to overcome the immense challenges that she faced by forgiving and achieving her purpose in life with unlimited generosity and kindness.

Life might have set unlimited obstacles and sorrows in your way, but they may reveal themselves to be not as big or as heavy as you have typically considered them to be. Remember that the dog that bites you in your imagination is always fiercer and more vicious that the one that is barking at you in real life. Sometimes fear and desperation don't allow us see the exit door that is opening before us. Faith and courage will help us to counter this scenario and to remember that we can always, always, find strength in our faith and in ourselves. Oftentimes, people are lost in their own pain feel and say that they have lost these qualities. Depression invades them and then hangs around like a shadow that accompanies them day and night; as a result, they can't see anything but that sadness. However, our strongest virtues aren't lost; they may be nascent, but they are always available to those who want to reestablish contact with them.

Obviously, all of us will have problems in our lives. These can be of a circumstantial or personal nature, relationship problems, health-related issues, or challenges related with material things, and they clearly bring us down, paralyze us, depress us, and make us sick, but if we know how to use them to our benefit, they teach us, deepen our understanding, put us in contact with our own innate wisdom, and finally elevate us. The great teachers and those who come to rise above their problems don't wonder, "why is this happening to me?" but rather, "what is the reason for this occurrence?" and they draw their conclusions from that place of inquiry rather than victimhood.

The famous saying, "what doesn't kill you makes you stronger," has a big hidden truth: choice. We can drown ourselves in suffering or come through it—that choice is a significant part of the human condition. Generally, people who successfully face their problems don't become paralyzed by concern or victimization; on the contrary, they look for happiness and gratitude. It isn't easy for them, but they practice it daily.

Always remember that there are many people who have endured tragedies and very difficult problems, yet they don't allow their past to become their jailer; through inner and conscious work, they succeeded in changing the paradigms that enabled them to stop always making the same paralyzing mistakes. Through such efforts, they can cure their wounds. I admire those people with deep fascination because they can transform their future into one filled with wellbeing and happiness, proving through their example that with a very particular combination of effort and inner work, it is possible to overcome, no matter the size of the trauma that you may have experienced in the past.

In the following chapters, I will illustrate with more detail the way that we can take control of our bodies and our emotions in order to start projecting the necessary changes that lead to a healthy, beautiful, and happy life. For now, I will close with this little story that the spiritual guide and Hindu/Jesuit priest, Anthony de Mello, used to tell: When asked about his enlightenment, the Master always remained reserved. The disciples tried all means to make him talk. All they knew was what was said on a certain occasion when the Master told his youngest son, who wanted to know how his father had felt when he reached enlightenment. The answer was: "like an idiot." When the boy asked why he felt this way, the Master answered: "well, you see, it was like making great effort to penetrate a house by climbing a wall and breaking a window, and only later realizing that the door was open the whole time."

CHAPTER 4

This is the "Plan"

While starting on my path towards personal healing, I realized that I was the only owner of my life, not anyone else. I found myself facing the decision of having to take the reins of my life into my own hands because no one else was going to do it for me. That moment of deep revelation opened my eyes to a new reality where I understood that my only hope was to trust myself and my innate capabilities.

When facing this truth, I recognized that I had two options: 1.) to keep living like a victim, blaming the circumstances, destiny, God, my family, etc. or 2.) to surrender to my disease and wait for my death. Neither of these two would've really healed me because even if I had chosen death, I would've left this world with a sad soul, filled with frustration and fears, instead of closing my eyes for the last time with a grateful spirit and at peace with my experience on Earth.

Deep down, I knew that I wanted to improve, in the same way that you know it also. Like you, I feared failing "one more time." Even if you look for thousands of excuses to deny yourself the possibility of wellbeing and liberation from what harms you, the basis of each excuse is always fear. Fear gets in the way of everything and paralyzes us. But there is a part inside of you that knows the truth. I understand that we all have negative thoughts occasionally—even daily— and that they are difficult to abandon because they are very real for us.

It isn't easy to trust our inner power when we think that we deserve "all of the bad things" that we are going through. It seems like we are convinced that we don't have enough value, and thus, even if we mustered the strength to try, surely the result would turn out wrong. I propose that you recognize that this is only a thought, a form of energy that is not solid but can be changed, modified, re-directed… You only have to choose a better thought and put it in the place of the negative one that is making you sick and draining your strength. Sometimes, this effort can take the form of a prayer or mantra. When you feel beaten, remember that there are many people who are going through similar or more complicated situations, and that despite this truth, you *can* get up every morning grateful for the new day.

I have worked with many cases and countless different problems, and I can assure you that the people who have achieved liberation aren't better than you, nor do they have more tools to face life—no more intelligence or power than you do. The only thing that has enabled them to cure themselves of their suffering is that they have made the decision to be the owners of their lives, and from that starting point, they move forward with the help of the universe that always conspires with us to help us reach our wellbeing.

Through my job and life itself, I learned that things don't change overnight— that everything has its time, and everything arrives on time. Generally, everything arrives just in the moment when we are truly prepared to take the next step. That is how this book has arrived in your hands now. While you read it, you might think that these are only pretty words, that you don't have the patience or dedication necessary to get better. Maybe you don't have the desire to fight. When I feel like this, the words of African American writer and activist, Frederick Douglas, inspire me: "Only the ones who fight win the battle."

It is very normal to feel poorly when you are tired, but you don't have to believe that the situation is not going to improve simply because, in that specific moment, your strength seems to yield to life's pressures. Even if you think that your resilience is a lie, if you meditate on it, you will realize that there is a huge sense of freedom in these situations when you feel that "you have lost it all." When you have nothing left to lose, whether it is due to a disease, separation, death, or a financial crisis, you have the incredible opportunity to choose freely and with no restraints. Thus, use the pieces of whatever has broken to build your new life based on what you have learned up until now.

We live in a world where everything seems to be "healed" with a pill. There are pills for everything, in all sizes, colors, and strengths. But there is no pill that offers patience or the will to find the inner power that enables you to truly heal your ailments without hiding their symptoms. This is something that you must arrive at through your own conscience and reflection. When I worked in the Family Conservation Department of the Kedren Psychiatric Hospital, I had the opportunity to assist several very terrible cases wherein most of the people were real victims. This department is an organization that offers short term services to help families in crisis through an improvement in the upbringing and operating of the household, with the goal of keeping children safe and sound. This service emerged from the recognition that kids need to grow in a stable and safe family. Family separation is a traumatic event that often leaves negative and lasting effects, and so the department works with children and their parents in their own homes, offering them the necessary services and tools to improve the situation. It was always very difficult for me to witness the suffering of so many kids, whom I consider true victims. But it's actually children, and not adults, who have the biggest possibilities for salvation because in their innocence, they still preserve faith, hope, and dreams of a better life.

I remember when I treated girls who had been repeatedly raped by family members. There was one in particular who touched my heart deeply. She was fourteen years old and had been the victim of abuse from her stepfather since she was seven. She had endured the pain in silence and fear, as her stepfather had threatened her to kill the whole family if she ever told. When she was twelve, though, the girl finally had the courage to tell her mother what was happening. The little girls suffered from severe depression, which caused her to mutilate herself and attempt to take her own life several times. She also had discipline problems at school, and she often ditched classes. I was able to help her a little with her depression and suicidal tendencies while she was in foster care, where I tended to her and her mother. Unfortunately, though, when she went returned to live with her mother, she stopped attending therapy, and I don't what happened to her. This was one of the saddest cases that I worked on because even I doubted that in cases such as this there was still a chance that this little girl could have a better life. At such a young age, my client had suffered so much that the logical consequence of all that had happened could have been taking her own life. Yet, at times, she had also shared her longing for a positive change and her hope of having a better life and being happy. She didn't know how to get there, but she still desired it, even if it seemed that there was no chance that this was going to happen.

I know that it might seem very hard, impossible even, to choose the option of change, but I also know that life is filled with opportunities and people willing to help you as soon as you make the determination that "yes, you can!" The saying, "when one door closes, another one opens," is not only true, but many times, two and three and four doors open all at the same time because the universe supports your decision of walking towards happiness and wellbeing.

I remember than when my health started to improve, I started feeling enthusiasm again. The joy of living overtook me, and I started to contemplate what I wanted to do now that I felt better. The options were many, but the ones that appealed to me most were either going back to my work or studying nutrition. I was passionate about the latter because I could see and feel the results of healing through food in my own body, and I wished to help other people so that they could benefit from such work too. Following this calling from deep within my heart, I contacted Meals on Wheels in Los Angeles about volunteering. This organization delivers meals to people who, because of disabilities or illness, can´t go shopping for groceries or cook their own food. The first day that I was to volunteer, I was not only late but also at the wrong address because there are several offices in Los Angeles. When I finally got to the office, the person in charge couldn't find my name on the list of volunteers and assumed that I must have been assigned to another office. Fortunately, a "coincidence" happened that that day, as that office was in need of more volunteers, so she put me to work with another person who had a similar professional background to me as a psychologist, but who recently had decided to change her profession and become a health coach. She told me all about this program, which I instantly felt in love with, as I realized that this was exactly what I wanted to do with my life. In that moment, I felt that my calling was to be a guide who would help people find their wellbeing through nourishment and lifestyle. It was as if

God had guided me precisely to the place where my mind and soul wanted to be.

During another opportunity, I treated a young mother with two little children, who had been taken by state because of the mother's drug use. This woman loved her children, and she was really trying to end her addiction. She attended rehabilitation and therapy, but shortly thereafter she was back on drugs. Her dependence was so deep that not even the love that she had for her children and from her children could save her. This case was particularly challenging for me because of the effect that the mother´s addiction had on the children who suffered the consequences as much, or more, than she did. Even though I still didn't have children at that time, I realized the huge power that we as parents have over our children, and how every gesture, every action, every choice that we make impacts their lives, and sometimes the lives of our grandchildren and great-grandchildren as well. I thought about my father and his alcoholism, of the physical abuse that I received as a result, of my mother's rejection of me. I also thought about all of the inner work that I was forced to do and that I keep doing to deal with the damage that such circumstances had done to me.

In the case of this addict mother, the only thing that

helped her to escape from the vicious circle that she was trapped in was mustering the determination from deep within herself to reclaim her life again. It´s true, she had been hurt and abused in the past, but nothing could change that, and even though she had tried to numb the suffering with drugs, these ultimately couldn't help her either. On the contrary, after a brief relief, they buried her more deeply in continual trauma. What she understood through therapy, though, was that even if her past couldn't be altered, her present and her future depended on her, and these parts could be modified according to her thoughts and actions.

I remembered the moment when I saw her become truly aware of this choice. We were in our usual session when she confessed that one of her kids had admitted to her that he was afraid that she would die, and that he and his brother would be taken to foster care forever. This forced her to face a cruel and likely reality: her kids could be left alone in this life, since the whereabouts of their father were unknown. In that moment, my client decided to change. It was simultaneously a difficult and rewarding path. I still keep in mind the day when this mother finally joined her children again, healthy, happy, and ready to start a new life.

I have chosen this case as an example to remind you that sometimes, we don't only harm ourselves with our behavior; we also harm those we love the most. Even if you think or feel that life isn't worth changing, if you focus on those whom love you and who you love back, you might find the strength that you need to take the first step and then keep moving forward. You change so those whom you love don't suffer. It is a good start, a good reason. Then you will see for yourself that this takes you to beautiful horizons that you never could have imagined when you were at the height of your problems and suffering.

Just as with the mother in my previous case, when I got sick, the fear of leaving my daughters without a mother was what drove me to find an alternative solution. When I saw their innocent faces, and their little hands caressed me with tenderness, I mustered the strength and courage to go on. I didn't want them to see me depressed all the time, sick and with no vitality. I realized that my suffering affected them a lot, as it made them sad and caused them to develop much insecurity. So, I made the effort, many times reluctantly, to smile, to move, to do things, to change. One day it was no longer an effort, and everything started flowing in a wonderful way that surprised even me. Maybe this is not the case for you, and you believe that you've got no one to fight for. That's ok, but I don't think that you want to spend the rest of your life drowning in the sea of your own suffering. I assure you that there is always,

always, a possibility to improve. Remember that as long as there is life, there is hope, and from hope, change can come. Merely desiring a better future can be the motivation that you need to start walking towards one. Don't worry; the rest flows readily if you are open to it.

These are only a couple of the many cases that I have treated. I imagine that you also know people who may have similar problems. These situations can happen even in the best families. And as I explained before, these kinds of mechanisms where the past becomes our prison not only happens to the poor and the ignorant, as many people think; any human being can be a victim of them.

Returning to the process that leads you to reclaiming your own life, many people cower at the thought of how much work they'll have to do, but the truth is that this transformation can become a wonderful inner journey, during which you will learn to know and respect yourself just as you are. The recovery of your self-esteem and the acceptance of your personal history (and of all the characteristics within you) will also reignite your power and provide you with the possibility of reaching the dreams that you may not even have dared to dream. That was the case for me, and now I thank my disease so much, for it opened my eyes and comprehension to be able to heal my body, mind, and soul once and for all. When I felt like I was dying, I learned to appreciate life, and I saw value in my health at the exact moment when I no longer had it. While I prayed for my recovery, I understood that for me, true happiness was enjoying good health. In that moment, I didn't care for the material things that surrounded me because without health, I couldn't enjoy anything, not even my family. Seeing them so worried and depressed because I was sick made me terribly sad. Conversely, the better I got, the bigger the happiness and light that sprouted from not only me, but also my family members and friends who felt so happy too. My life was unfolding in a way that I had never experienced before. I woke up every morning with joy, and I thanked God for a new day and a new chance to improve. I started to see life as a gift from God that is meant to be enjoyed in every moment; we never know when it's going to end, so why go around suffering and indulging in negative thoughts and emotions? Indeed, my illness proved to me that even the hardest moments hide a gift.

It is still wonderful to wake up every day with the desire and the enthusiasm to start a new adventure while counting on a source of inner strength that was unknown to me before, but which looks after me and protects me so that I don't make the same mistakes again. By saying "Yes!" to life, I launched myself into situations that I never would've dared to try for fear of failure, such as resting during the day without feeling guilty about caring for myself, forgiving, going back to school, opening my own business, learning to swim and ski, giving lectures to hundreds of people, visiting other countries, and even allowing myself to write this book! I honestly believe that this is only the beginning, and I can assure you that I am no more a miracle than you are. We all have the possibility of choosing. As oppressed as you may feel, the possibility still exists for you to change your life. When you embrace the process of acquiring self-knowledge and healing, it's as if you have suddenly returned to infancy. When you were little, you encountered everything as an extraordinary discovery. You were never bored. You used to trust yourself and the world around you. So, when you decide return to who you really are, you start finding things in yourself that you didn't even remember are there—things like faith, hope, enthusiasm… Things like dreams that you buried in order to silence them and keep them from hurting you because you thought that you would never achieve them. The great thing is that with every step that you take, you realize that each one of those dreams presents a possibility of realization. The writer Richard Bach says in his book Illusions, "You are never given a wish without also being given the power to make it true. You might have to work for it, however."

This and so many other quotes have helped me a lot in my process, which is why I have decided to include them throughout this book— in hopes that they may also illuminate you. When you start learning stories of other people who have achieved positive change in their lives and who haven't given up at the hands of defeat, but have accepted it with dignity and have started over, such knowledge gives you immense strength. I am going to tell you a story that I read some years ago:

The eagle is a magnificent animal that lives around 70 years. When the eagle enters its forties, it is forced to make a very hard, life-or-death decision. At this age, her nails are so curved that they are no longer useful for capturing the prey that she needs in order to feed. Her beak also curves in such a way that she can no longer drink water nor eat. Her wings start sticking to her chest because the feathers are too long and heavy, making it very difficult to fly. So, the eagle is faced with two options: die or face a 150-day process of transformation. The eagle opts for the second choice, and with her last strength flies to a very high mountain, where she finds shelter near a wall. Once she finds this spot, the eagle beats her beak against the wall until she reaps it off.

Upon doing so, she must wait patiently until a new beak grows, and she will then use it to take her nails off. Stripped of her old beak and nails, which have been replaced by new ones, she proceeds to take off her old feathers. When the new feathers grow back, she is now once again ready for a new flight. It is said that this is the best flight for an eagle, as it is the one that she has been preparing for her whole life. It is the flight of restoration and majesty. When the eagle abandons the mountain that has served as her shelter, she is ready for her new life.

Some don't believe that this is a true story; some do. I have chosen to use it in this book as a source of inspiration for you, beyond scientific evidence about the life of eagles.

I also love this story because I have entered my forties, and I relate to the eagle. Like her, I also decided to rip my old feathers out and spread my new wings. And during this flight, I want to share with you some of my tools that have helped me to not only free myself personally, but to also assist my clients. This toolbox is a guide to light, a plan that I have developed for the benefit of all of you…. I have called it PlanPluz.

It is a "plan" because it has several elements that in a coordinated way will help you to achieve the result that you want: to free yourself from your past, from all the burdens in order to be happy, to live better, and to conquer your dreams and enjoy everything that you have fought for and deserve.

It goes even beyond that, though; this plan has a "plus," and that plus is that it connects your body and your soul, yourself with your environment and with those who surround you. We often think that the change has to be physical or spiritual, but it actually has to embrace both for the change to be complete. It also isn't enough that the change is internal because for a real change to happen, it has be to reflected and projected onto others.

This "plus" has a very special hallmark with a lot of "light" ("luz" in Spanish), which is how it has become "Pluz." This change is not only because that is my name, for at this point you might've realize that ego is not one of the characteristics of my personality... I named it as such because this plan has been a light that drove me towards the path of physical and spiritual peace and lightened the exit of the prison where I had been living. From the bottom of my heart, I hope that it does the same for you—that it assists you in discovering your own sacred wellbeing.

"It is now forbidden not to smile in the face of adversity; to stop fighting for what you want; to abandon it all because of your fears; or to give up in making your own dreams come true." Pablo Neruda

Let's get to work!

As a first step, it is important that you understand the intimate connection that exists between your body and your mind: if the body is not healthy and peaceful, the mind suffers the consequences and vice versa. Emotions are also altered if the body and mind suffer from imbalances.

It was hard for me to become aware of the mind-body connection because even when I worked with people who had emotional and mental difficulties, I didn't relate the problems of the body with emotions and mental state, and I know that there are many people who don't believe that there is a bond that unites them. My comprehension expanded when it was time to realign my own mind and balance my own emotions in order to be able to heal my body. No healing or medicine would've worked without this intersection of mind, body, spirit. Strong emotional health consists of feeling good about ourselves, controlling our own thoughts, and not letting them control us. When you feel good emotionally, you can put problems into perspective instead of letting them drown you; you also maintain better communication with people, and, in general, your energy keeps flowing in a positive way, even if your life circumstances aren't the ones that you desire in that moment.

If emotions are balanced, it is very hard for the mind to get sick. However, there are some afflictions of the mind that have their origin in physical instabilities. For example, some chemical imbalances localized in the brain can impact physical health. But people who have relatively strong emotional wellbeing can overcome these problems much faster and even avoid or prevent them because they quickly realize that something isn't working right as soon they feel the first symptoms, which, in many occasions, are very subtle.

The bigger the success that I experienced in my healing process, the greater my curiosity to study and corroborate what I was learning in my own body. For example, one of the studies that greatly appealed me was conducted by the School of Medicine and Dentistry faculty at the University of Rochester, where the psychologist Robert Ader discovered that the nervous and immune systems have a very important bond that allows that mind, emotions, and body to communicate. One of the things that Ader noticed was that negative emotions, like depression, rage, stress, and anxiety, among others, produce chemicals and hormones that, with time, deteriorate the functioning of the immune system, leaving the body more vulnerable to diseases.[1]

Throughout several studies published in his book, Psychoneuroimmunology, Ader demonstrated how living for long periods with chronic anxiety, sadness, negativity, continuous stress, mistrust, fear, and anger can be the detonators that trigger diseases, such as rheumatoid arthritis, cardio-pulmonary conditions, obesity, headaches, stomach ulcers, and fibromyalgia, to develop in our bodies. So, to help you prevent these ailments, I am going to share with you what I found particularly useful: a method that I developed throughout the years when addressing my own issues, and which I use in my own consultations with successful results in my patients' lives as well. In addition, I invite you to keep on studying and finding the tools that are most useful to you to enhance your own healing.

PlanPluz is very easy to remember. I developed it this way because very often people don't have time to study different techniques that require complicated efforts and routines that are impossible to follow. My advice is

[1]   Robert   Ader,   Nicholas   Cohen,   David   Felten. "Psychoneuroimmunology: Interactions Between The Nervous System and The Immune System." The Lancet 345 (1995) 99-103

simple and easy to put into practice. If you commit and exercise the practices that I lay out, I assure you that they can free you from your prison and finally help you find the happiness that you so desire. I call these tools The ABC's:

- Add Movement

- Be Grateful

- Cherish your Body

Add Movement

One of the consequences that I suffered as a result of having a low white blood cell count was rheumatoid arthritis, an ailment that affects movement of the joints and other parts of the body. It causes pain, swelling, and stiffness, usually in more than one place. This disease causes a lot of physical pain and fatigue, and sometimes you can even develop a fever. When I couldn't stand the pain and inflammation, one of the rheumatologists that I visited advised me to start doing physical exercise. This surprised me because I could barely move, and I couldn't imagine exercising while suffering from so much pain. In the past I had done physical activity sporadically, but I had never related it to healing an affliction. I thought that it was useful for losing weight, forming, muscles, or gaining flexibility, and to be honest, in that moment, exercising my body was the furthest thought from my mind.

I remember as clearly as if it were yesterday when the doctor told me something that exercise was very important for me: if I did so, the pain was going to be bad, but if I didn't, it would be worse. That day, I left the doctor's office more disappointed than ever. My mind couldn't focus on anything; I just felt the pain in my body and all of the different symptoms that were causing me so much discomfort and inconvenience. Despite my problems, though, I didn't want to give up, so I started reading and learning about the benefits of physical activity for people with arthritis and imbalances of the immune system.

One article, published by the American College of Rheumatology, spoke about the importance of physical exercise for people with arthritis, stating, among other things, that "arthritis is one of the most common reasons people give for limiting physical activity and recreational pursuits. Inactivity, in addition to arthritis-related problems, can result in a variety of health risks, including Type II diabetes, cardiovascular disease and osteoporosis. In addition, decreased pain tolerance, weak muscles, stiff joints and poor balance common to many forms of arthritis can be made worse by inactivity. For many older people with arthritis, joint and muscle changes due to aging can make matters worse. Therefore, for the person with arthritis, the right kind of exercise is very important."[2]

So, despite my pain, I started investigating the best exercises for people who suffer from rheumatoid arthritis, one of which is yoga. The word 'Yoga' comes from Sanskrit and means "union." It is the practice of a set of bodily positions combined with specific breathing, the goal of which is to find the union between body, mind, and spirit. Though I considered all of the most popular types of yoga (Hatha, Kundalini, Iyengar, Ashtanga, and Bikram), it was recommended that practice Yoga nidra, which has two significant benefits for fighting rheumatoid arthritis: using deep relaxation techniques that promote a healthy immune system and reduce the inflammation in the joints, combined with soft stretching exercises that maintain movement fluency. The practice of yoga in general has countless benefits. According to the International Association of Yoga Therapists, among the positive effects of yoga on the body, you will find that it creates

---

[2] "Exercise and Arthritis," <u>American College of Rheumatology</u>, 2015, rheumatology.org <u>https://www.rheumatology.org/i-am-a/patient-caregiver/diseases-conditions/living-well-with-rheumaticdisease/exercise-and-arthritis</u>

"stable autonomic nervous system equilibrium... pulse rate decreases, respiratory rate decreases, blood pressure decreases... cardiovascular efficiency increases, respiratory efficiency increases... gastrointestinal function normalizes, endocrine function normalizes ... musculoskeletal flexibility and joint range of motion increase, posture improves, strength and resiliency increase, endurance increases, energy level increases, weight normalizes, sleep improves, immunity increases, pain decreases."[3]

In a study conducted by the Indian Institute of Technology, Roorkee, men between the ages of 18 and 48 were studied to investigate the benefits of yoga on cardiac health. By the end of the experiment, electrocardiograms demonstrated that "the heart rate variability in yogic practitioners has shown to be higher than the subjects who do not practice yoga."[4] This means that the yoga practitioners had good regulation of the cardiac intervals that are controlled by the autonomous nervous system compared to those who

---

[3] Trisha Lamb, "Healthy Benefits of Yoga," The International Association of Yoga Therapists, 2004, http://www.iayt.org.

[4] Sunkaria, Ramesh., Kumar, Vinod., et al., "A comparative Study of on Spectral Parameters of Heart Rate Variability in Yogi and Non-Yogi Practitioners," Journal of Medical Engineering and Informatics 2 (2010): 1-14

don't practice. This implies that the latter group had a higher risk of having arrhythmias and hearts disorders.

Many people think that yoga is a religious practice, but it isn't; it is a discipline linked to spirituality, and people of any religion can practice it. So, with immense effort, I took up yoga, even though I couldn't sit down for more than five minutes without feeling unbearable pain. Now I know that at this point in my life, my body and I weren't yet prepared to benefit from this wonderful discipline. It unsettled me to remain sitting because I was too worried about what was going on with my body. My focus was on my pain and my disease, so I had a hard time focusing on breathing, and I certainly couldn't relax. I also felt frustrated because after trying several yoga sessions, my pain hadn't diminished; on the contrary, I felt it even deeper. At times, I was inspired and perhaps even envious when I heard my classmates speak about how good they felt after each session, but this ultimately left me sadder and disappointed because once more, I had failed in the attempt. So I decided to leave yoga until I was ready. Currently, I practice it successfully, and I enjoy it immensely because it helps me to reduce daily stress. Maybe, as it happened to me, yoga is not for you— maybe not yet, or maybe not ever. Don't be discouraged, though; there are hundreds of physical activities with which you can connect. The important thing is not to give up and to instead keep trying. That was what I did, and, following my doctor´s suggestion, I tried Pilates.

Pilates places a lot of emphasis on breathing and the alignment of the spine. The exercises are practiced in a slow, soft, and controlled way. This method is usually recommended for people with pre-existing injuries, backaches, arthritis, tension, and muscular problems because through its practice, you can re-educate the body to improve your posture and movement. Pilates is also very good for reducing stress. It was created in the beginning of the 20th century by the German Joseph Hubertus, and it consists of a series of physical exercises focused on fortifying and toning the muscles without increasing their volume. Besides training your body, it also focuses on the mind. Several studies on Pilates have found that, among its numerous benefits, you can improve alignment, symmetry, and awareness of your own body, in addition to gaining better control over your mental state as well. Through conscious perception of how one's body feels and how its posture is, the person learns to relate these habits to the pains and injuries that plague him or her.

In a twelve-week study done by the Sport Sciences Faculty of the University of Castilla-La Mancha, it was concluded that even if the expected results were initially that the subjects would improve their form, become acquainted with the activity, and improve their levels of strength and flexibility, by practicing said method for twelve weeks in three ninety-minute sessions per week, the participants noted the following benefits: greater awareness of their incorrect posture habits, an improvement in their levels of flexibility, and decreased backaches. Other smaller benefits were the use of Pilates in the practice of sports and cosmetic benefits. However, regarding these last ones, there are significant differences observed in the anthropometric data before and after the program.[5]

While it can be very beneficial, there may be also people for whom Pilates doesn't work. Maybe the classes are too quiet if you are looking or something that has a faster rhythm, or you simply don't feel comfortable using the necessary Pilates equipment. During my sessions, my pain got worse, and I thought that I wasn't doing it right because I couldn't keep up with the group. I believed that the problem was me, and not the activity itself. I then decided to make a sacrifice and hire a personal trainer, but I still struggled with strong pain that worsened in sessions. Once again, my own worries

---

[5] Teresa, G. Pastor, Susana A. Lain, "Pilates Method: Changes in Body Composition and Spinal Flexibility in Healthy Adults," Apunts Medicina de l'Esport, 46 (2011): 17-22

kept me from the necessary patience that is required to experience the benefits. The trainer explained to me that at the beginning of the practice, I would need to learn how to wait and be consistent. I was also reassured that I wasn't the problem, and that it is very common for the progress to be slow. But how could I keep going with something that increased my pain instead of helping me? When I considered the pain that I suffered while driving, the high price of classes, the cost of childcare for my daughters, and the absence of any marked improvement, I didn't really see the reward. Again, my hopes plummeted, and I was invaded by frustration because even if I tried with all of my strength, I didn't see or feel any results. I completely empathize with people who try again and again to improve their health, their relationships, their professional lives with hope, only to feel they aren't garnering any results. I understand your frustration and disenchantment. I also understand the fact that at a certain point, you surrender, for fear of continued failure. I lived this reality myself when neither medicine nor exercise worked. However, I kept going. I thought that if the answer to my problem was in adding some kind of movement, then I simply couldn't give up.

The experts also recommended swimming as a very effective exercise to fight rheumatoid arthritis. The Arthritis Foundation informs us that, "warm water therapy works wonders for all kinds of musculoskeletal conditions, including fibromyalgia, arthritis and low back pain… It makes you feel better. It makes the joints looser. It reduces pain and it seems to have a somewhat prolonged effect that goes beyond the period of immersion… Warm water is great for relaxing, but it is also good for moving. Warm water stimulates blood flow to stiff muscles and frozen joints, making a warm tub or pool an ideal place to do some gentle stretching… Warm water can be so helpful in fighting the pain and stiffness of arthritis and fibromyalgia that experts recommend heated pools for exercise. Various studies of patients with both conditions found that when they participated in warm water exercise programs two or three times a week, their pain decreased as much as 40 percent and their physical function increased. The exercise programs also gave an emotional boost, helped people sleep better and were particularly effective for obese individuals."[6] Unfortunately, at that point in time, I didn't know how to swim. I also tried, in vain, different types of physical therapies with several personal trainers because the pain kept getting worse. Ultimately, however, I abandoned

---

[6] "Warm Water Works Wonders on Pain," Arthritis Foundation, http://www.arthritis.org/living-with-arthritis/pain-management/tips/warm-water-therapy.php

them.

I spent some time continuing to move from frustration to frustration, until I met my holistic healer who advised me to try some physical activities that I enjoyed. I have always liked music and dancing, but my body was in too much pain to dance, and I was afraid that I might hurt myself even more. The other option was walking. I have always loved to walk— maybe because when I was little, I walked everywhere. I told my healer, and he then suggested something that he called "Walking Meditation." The New Zealander Eric Harrison, known for his work with meditation, is confident in the successes that can be achieved by meditating while we walk, so I decided to try it for myself. It seemed like something very simple that I could do alone, at my own pace, and I didn't have to pay for lessons or use any equipment or accessories. I could simply enjoy my surroundings and listen to music while I did it. In the beginning, I couldn't walk more than five minutes without getting to the point where I couldn't stand the pain, but I really enjoyed being outside. I enjoyed the view, the beauty of the day, the sun. When I added gratitude while I walked, everything started becoming more bearable, even the pain. And even if I wasn't recovering as fast as I would've liked, my mood was improving, and this gave me faith and trust in the process that I had started to grow each day.

Simply enjoying nature and the Los Angeles sun made me very happy. I was very relaxed just being outdoors. I felt the freedom of choosing between listening to music, praying, and thanking God for my life experience, and this was very comforting.

Finally, my mind found the tranquility that it desperately needed and instead of stewing in my pain and problems, I focused on the beauty, the flow of movement, my feet touching the ground, the soft sway of my arms, the temperature of the air, and the natural sounds. This literally allowed my mind to get out of the way, thereby enabling my body to put in practice its innate powers of self-healing. I started with five minutes, then moved to ten, fifteen, and, little by little, to thirty! The more I walked, the more relaxed I felt, and my strength grew slowly but surely. With time, I noticed that the pain in my joints lessened, and my mood improved, and this progress gave me the encouragement to continue. When I started to have concrete proof of my healing, walking became a daily activity, and I learned many things about the benefits of walking for a good health, among them:

- It´s free, and you can do it anywhere and at the time of the day that best suits you.

- You don´t need devices, extra elements, or a teacher who guides you. Just you and a good pair of shoes can do the job.

- Walking is comfortable at any age, and each person can find his or her path beyond the physical or emotional condition that afflicts him or her.

- It improves your circulatory system.

- It can decrease your weight.

- It balances your cholesterol.

- It helps you to maintain healthy blood pressure.

- It detoxes your body.

- It regulates your breathing.

- It strengthens your legs and naturally reduces your belly fat.

- It exercises your heart.

- It combats cellulite and flabbiness.

- It relaxes you and eases your tension.

- It combats depression.

- It clears your mind and enhances your creativity.

The director of the Investigation of Sports and Health Division at the University of Valencia and expert of the General Council of the Official Schools of Physical Education and Physical Activities Sciences and Sports Graduates, Juan Carlos Colado Sánchez, asserts that, "systematically walking can improve the physical form, and being fit considerably reduces the premature risk of sickness and/or death. Even humble increases in the physical conditions of sedentary people are associated with significant benefits."[7]

An article published by Europe PubMed Central mentioned a set of studies that arrived at the conclusion that walking is beneficial in several aspects that help one to reach optimum health status: "Walking as a healthful form of physical activity began to receive attention in the 1990s due to new recommendations that emphasized moderate-intensity physical activity. The main example of moderate-intensity activity in the 1995 Centers for Disease Control/American College of

---

[7] Medrano, Ivan. "Actividad de los Músculos Para Vertebrales Durante Ejercicios que Requieran Estabilidad Raquidea." Universidad de Valencia: Departamento de Educación Física y Deportiva, 2011: www.tesisenred.net/bitstream/handle/10803/81393/chulvi.pdf

Sports Medicine recommendation was brisk walking at 3 to 4 mph. Evidence for the health benefits of walking comes largely from epidemiologic studies. When interpreting the data from such studies, it is necessary to consider several methodological issues, including the design of the study, confounding by other lifestyle behaviors, and confounding by other kinds of physical activity. Walking has the potential to have a large public health impact due to its accessibility, its documented health benefits, and the fact that effective programs to promote walking already exist."[8] This same report concluded that, "Walking is a simple health behavior that can reduce rates of chronic disease and ameliorate rising health care costs, with only a modest increase in the number of activity-related injuries."[9]

In another study conducted by Doctor Marc Berman, psychiatrist of the Rotman Research Institute in Toronto, Canada, the research concluded that walking in a park, or in any natural environment surrounded by greenery, improves the cognitive functions of people

---

[8] Lee, I-Min and David Buchner., "The Importance of Walking to Public Health," Journal of Medicine and Science in Sports and Exercises 40 (2008): S 512-518
https://www.ncbi.nlm.nih.gov/pubmed/18562968

[9] Lee and Buchner 512

who suffer from depression. [10] Volunteers for this study were men and women who averaged twenty-six years of age and who suffered from depression. Each participant alternated between a walk in a park full of greenery and one in an urban, noisy environment. The research team concluded that walking in nature can complement or improve the existing treatments for clinical depression.[11] When you walk outdoors, you also nurture yourself with vitamin D, which is very important for the health of bones, the heart, and blood vessels. Vitamin D improves skin disorders, diabetes, obesity, muscular weakness, multiple sclerosis, and rheumatoid arthritis, among other things. It is also used to prevent cancer and autoimmune disease. The best source of vitamin D is the sun, and people who are not exposed to the sun in moderate quantities have a greater risk of Vitamin D deficiency.

I was surprised to learn about this, as many people like me during this time in my life have no awareness about how the sun helps to fortify the immune system. I am sure that this was one of the key elements in my body's

[10] Berman, Marc., John, Jonides., et al., "The Cognitive Benefits of Interacting with Nature." Journal of Psychological Science 19 (2008): 1207-1212

[11] Berman, John and Kaplan 1207-1212

recovery process. Now, I don't mean to suggest that you lay out in sun for hours, which can be harmful to your health and the opposite of what you want to achieve, but ten minutes of exposure per day is enough to receive the benefits. Unfortunately, our medical system doesn't regularly provide this information to patients, and it is fundamental knowledge because nowadays people spend a lot of time indoors at work, and even kids are on their computers all day when not at school. I wonder if this has influenced the increase in diseases we´ve experienced as a population.

Physical exercise in general contributes to the rehabilitation of health, the prevention of diseases, and the maintenance of harmony between mind, body, and emotions. Besides, exercise is way of investing in your health that has a low cost and is easy. In a study done by Girona University in Spain, researchers worked with several groups of people (young and old, male and female) and concluded that: "prescription of physical exercise is useful especially to prevent premature mortality of any cause, restricted blood supply to tissues, cerebrovascular disease, arterial hypertension, colon and breast cancer, type II diabetes, metabolic syndrome, obesity, osteoporosis, sarcopenia, functional dependency, falls in elders, cognitive deterioration, anxiety, and depression."[12]

The same study also explains that being in good shape means being able to do activities with energy, without fatigue, and with enjoyment, and it suggests that the most relevant components are the resistance, flexibility, and balance that are acquired with regular practice of movement. The experts that participated in this clinical study concurred on the great importance of physical activity as a mean of preventing diseases and premature mortality. In another report published by the European Council of Information on Alimentation, professor Ken Fox of Bristol University in the United Kingdom spoke about numerous studies that share the same results: that physical activity, especially when practiced by adults and elderly individuals, doubles one's possibility of avoiding a serious disease and premature death, while also preserving mental and emotional health. The report outlines how the benefits of practicing physical activity are as good for the body as the ones you get when you quit smoking.[13] Professor

---

[12] Bayego, E., Vila, G., et al., "Prescripción de Ejercicios Físico." Medicina Clínica 138 (2012): 18-24

[13] Fox, Kenneth., "Physical Activity and Mental Health Promotion: The Natural Partnership." Journal of Public Mental Health 2 (2006): 4-12

Fox himself drew conclusions from another study that, "sufficient evidence now exists for the effectiveness of exercise in the treatment of clinical depression. Additionally, exercise has a moderate reducing effect on state and trait anxiety and can improve physical self-perceptions and in some cases global self-esteem. Also there is now good evidence that aerobic and resistance exercise enhances mood states, and weaker evidence that exercise can improve cognitive function (primarily assessed by reaction time) in older adults … Together, this body of research suggests that moderate regular exercise should be considered as a viable means of treating depression and anxiety and improving mental well-being in the general public."[14]

In case you are still not convinced about the benefits of physical activity, take into consideration that if you want to lead a healthy life, exercise is fundamental because it promotes the production of antibodies, which are a kind of protein produced by the immune system to help the body combat viruses and maintain good health in general. Exercise also boosts your mood and helps you to acquire better self-esteem. While you are practicing physical activity, your body pushes

---

[14] Fox, Kenneth., "The Influence of Physical Activity on Mental Well-Being." Public Health Nutrition 2(3a) (1999): 411-418

endorphins to your brain. Endorphins are neuro-peptides (small protein chains) that are released through the spinal chord and the bloodstream and have special tasks, including promoting calmness, creating a generalized state of wellness, improving your mood, delaying the aging process, enhancing the immune system, and counteracting high levels of adrenaline associated with anxiety.

The reality is that as we grow old, our bodies weaken. Physical activity helps to keep our bodies strong and our minds active. Personally, I thank physical activity because it helped me to:

- Improve my health

- Improve my shape and physical fitness.

- Maintain a good weight.

- Improve and increase the tone and strength of my muscles.

- Increase my capability for moment in a progressive way.

- Make my joints more flexible and achieve better mobility.

In terms of psychological wellbeing, it helped me to:

- Increase my self-esteem.

- Be less socially isolated.

- Make me more confident with my own image.

- Reduce depression, tension, and stress.

- Improve the development of my personality.

- Improve my emotional state.

- Improve my mood in general.

Because of all of the above, I highly recommend physical exercise. It also made me aware of the value of my own effort and helped me to trust in the possibility of improvement for my health. It increased my self-esteem and, at the same time, filled me with energy and strength. I also learned that we are the ones who have control over our bodies and not the other way around, and that the limitations that cause us pain, obesity, and a sedentary life can be overcome if we put our intention behind it. The important thing for each of you is that you find a kind of movement that you enjoy. One of the reasons why many people stop doing exercise— including me at the beginning of my healing process— is that they view it as a mandatory task, and not as something that is fun, bearable, and good for their health. This is why you must choose the physical activity that is best for you, whether it is swimming, aerobics, yoga, independent, or group exercises. Variety of exercise is important, and there are workouts for all tastes and abilities. Numerous studies have confirmed that people who practice an exercise that they enjoy have more opportunities to do it than those who do it out of obligation. My advice is that while you are searching, you start with a simple practice like walking. That way, you can start training your body so that you feel in shape if you want to join a class or a gym. The most important thing is that you move because the more you do it, the happier you´ll be, and your general wellbeing will increase as a result.

There is an adaptation of a popular story written by Eloy Moreno that I usually recommend to my clients when they tell me that they can´t believe that they can actually start an exercise program, whether it´s because they feel sick, tired, overweight, or depressed. The story goes like this:

All morning, two kids had been skating on a frozen lake when suddenly, the ice broke and one of them fell into the water. The current pushed him a few feet underneath the frozen ice, so to save him, the only option was breaking the layer that was covering him. His friend started screaming for help, but seeing that nobody was nearby, he quickly searched for a stone and started hitting the ice with all of his strength. He pummeled the ice over and over until finally a crack appeared, through which he slipped his arm to grab his friend and save him. A few minutes later, called by the neighbors who had heard the cries for help, the fire department arrived. When they told the rescue team what had happened, the firemen couldn't stop asking themselves how this little boy had been able to break such a thick layer of ice. It seemed impossible that he had achieved it with his small hands because he couldn't possibly have enough strength. How could he do it? An elderly man, hearing this conversation, approached the firemen.

"I know how he did it," he said.

"How?" they asked, amazed.

"There was no one around him to tell him that he couldn't do it."

Be Grateful

As my body healed, I thanked God endlessly for my health. And the greater my gratitude, the bigger the reward that God gave me with improved health every day. When we are living in gratitude and express our thankfulness, we develop a mechanism wherein material (and this includes good health) and spiritual abundance start to vibrate in unison with our breathing. It´s as if everything in creation starts to take part in our day-to-day doings, and success starts to manifest itself. I once read an article in *The Guardian* newspaper that mentioned a nurse who took note of the "most common regrets of the dying." They are:

- I wish I'd had the courage to live a life true to myself, not the life others expected of me.

- I wish I hadn't worked so hard.

- I wish I'd had the courage to express my feelings.

- I wish I had stayed in touch with my friends.

- I wish that I had let myself be happier.[15]

When I finished reading this list of wishes, I felt very sad because in the moments when I was so sick that I thought I would die, I also had these regrets, especially

---

[15] Steiner, Susie, "Top Five Regrets of the Dying," The Guardian, February 2, 2012.
theguardian.com
https://www.theguardian.com/lifeandstyle/2012/feb/01/top-five-regrets-of-the-dying

the wish that "I had let myself be happier." We often lose the ability to be thankful for everything that we take for granted. Our families and friends, our possessions and jobs, our bodies, our feelings—we believe that these things will always be there for us—or we at least want to believe this. But it's not true. One of the thousands of things that I thank my disease for is teaching me that life is short, and it can disappear at any moment. Our lives are a gift from God—one that isn't given twice—and we must know how to seize it. When I realized this, I started to live in a state of complete gratitude, and soon I experienced the sheer beauty of thanking God every morning for the ability to keep fighting, even if my body was still sick and sore. I thought of how many people, unfortunately, no longer had this chance to persist, and I thanked God for the new day, for the strength to keep going, for the presence of an amazing husband, who, beyond cultural and language differences, was still by my side for more than twenty years, for my two beautiful, healthy, happy daughters. I realized how lucky I was, and I felt complete for the first time in my life.

The thing is that gratitude is born when we stop taking things for granted and start appreciating them as if "it was the only time we were going to have them." When we do, suddenly everything becomes valuable, including our own lives. In that moment, we value who we really are, and we also recognize the value in others. While I experimented with gratitude, I realized that even if my problems still existed, they were lighter, and the burden that they represented was more bearable and easy to deal with. The larger the gratitude that I felt for life, the greater the results that made my problems gradually disappear.

While I was self-healing, I sometimes had the feeling that the world also received a little bit of that healing. Now I can assure you that this is true. I´ve had more than enough proof that when you heal yourself, the world heals with you. The anxiety that my daughters indirectly experienced while seeing their mother sick healed with me, and at the same time, they did better in their relationships with their friends. The same was true for my husband. Once he had fewer worries, he could focus better on his job, and his company received the benefits that expanded to the consumers of the company´s products, and so on to infinity.

It's like when you throw a stone into a quiet lake and see how the waves get wider and wider as they move away from where the stone landed. Your happiness and gratitude are a pebble that has a great ripple effect on others' lives and the world at large. An analysis made by the *Journal of Personality and Social Psychology* shows that, "gratitude appears to build friendships and other social bonds. These are social resources because, in times of need, these social bonds are wellsprings to be tapped for the provision of social support. Gratitude, thus, is a form of love, a consequence of an already formed attachment as well as a precipitating condition for the formation of new affectional bonds"[16] Gratitude is like a muscle: the more you exercise it, the more it develops and the stronger it becomes inside of you. I know that it is usually difficult to be grateful in the darkest moments of life, but if you practice gratitude, you will see how the storm passes, making way for a beautiful rainbow and a new morning.

In my practice of gratitude, I am aware that every experience in my life—both the ones that I enjoy and the ones that cause me pain, sadness, or any other negative emotion—has been manifested for my own growth. When you appreciate life, you realize that it is not a coincidence or a mistake that you are on this Earth; you have a purpose. So, if you want to enjoy life and make the most of it, you must find your purpose, your mission for this existence. In my case, I have always wanted to help others, and appreciation and

---

[16] Robert A. Emmons and Michael E. McCullough, "Counting Blessings vs. Burden: An Experimental Investigation of Gratitude and Subjective Well-Being in Daily Life" Journal of Personality and Social Psychology, 84 (2003): 377-389

gratitude offer me the drive to keep going.

Upon adding the practice of gratitude, increased movement, and a change in diet to the agenda for my healing, I realized that my purpose in life is guiding others towards their personal freedom by helping them to live happy and healthy lives. This was the reason why I went back to school to study nutrition and decided to write this book: to have a positive and multiplying impact on a greater number of people. My dream is to keep delivering a message of health and wellness to the whole world, as when we realize that we have a reason for living, we become thankful, happy, and open to new possibilities. Our spirits raise, and our hearts fill with compassion.

Suddenly, things that have seemed incomprehensible make sense. We learn to appreciate what we have instead of whining about what we don't. Envy vanishes before a grateful heart. Gratitude lets us know that even unpleasant things that enter our lives are helping us to grow. Such thoughts can bring a lot of mental and emotional peace because you realize that there are no mistakes or bad luck. Everything that happens contributes to continuous learning and has a reason for occurring. In order to feel grateful, many people expect good fortune to come knocking at their doors, but in reality, gratitude is a constant practice of life. If you don't exercise it often, you won't do so when things go right. When I feel that "everything is going wrong," I express gratitude for the things that are going to be fixed "in no time." If I have no money, I am thankful for any funds that soon will come to me. When my health falters, I am thankful for a recovery that is on its way. In moments of loneliness, I thank my friends and family, and even if they are not present in that moment, I am thankful that they are a part of my life and my history.

At this point, I am going to tell you a children´s story that I love because it clarifies the power of gratitude:

There once was a lion that, after a long day of hunting, laid down to rest. While his eyes were heavily closing, a mouse wandered by and tripped on the lion´s mane, waking the lion up. The enraged beast held the mouse between his paws and asked, "How dare you wake me, you tiny creature?! I will show you no mercy and eat you so that you don´t bother me anymore!"

The mouse, terrified, begged, "Lion, please, don't hurt me. I will be forever grateful if you let me go, and you will always be able to count on me for whatever you need! Who knows, someday you might need my help." The mouse begged so earnestly that finally the lion let him go. Years went by, and one day as the mouse was

111

walking through the jungle, he heard roars filled with pain and anguish. He hurried towards the source of the noise, for he had recognized the voice of the lion that once spared his life. He soon found the poor beast, trapped in a hunting net. "Don´t worry lion!" he said. "I'll save you!" And to the lion´s surprise, the little mouse started gnawing each one of the ropes that trapped the beast until he was finally free. "I told you my gratitude was eternal!" said the mouse to the thankful lion. "When we are thankful, we always find freedom," the mouse continued. And from that day on, lions and mice have been friends that always help each other when the need arises.

It is a simple story for small children, but it offers great wisdom. You don't achieve gratitude by taking a pill or dieting or working hard. Gratitude is a conscious practice that is as simple as the lion´s story. It is born from the appreciation of small things, the moments that make up a day, the days that make up a week, the weeks that make up a month… and when you work at it, it becomes a part of your good daily habits. It can´t be forced, but it is a choice—something that emerges when we consciously choose to focus on the blessings that every situation offers. When things get hard, I like to ask God: "Please, help me to see the good in this situation," or "help me to find the positive side and learn from this experience." Maybe the problem will still be there, or maybe it will be fixed, but the important thing is that by feeling gratitude for the positive in each situation, I grow and improve; my heart and understanding open up, and in the end, despite the challenges, I usually feel happy.

Once while I was doing Internet research for a lecture that I had to give about gratitude, I found an anecdote that I was extremely resonant. It was about the English minister and biblical commentator Matthew Henry, who lived between 1662 and 1714. On one occasion, the minister was robbed and when his friends and colleagues asked him how he was, he answered that he felt very grateful. This of course surprised everyone he told, but he then explained that he thanked God deeply because firstly, it was the first time that he was robbed; secondly, they had only stolen only a bag and left him unharmed; thirdly, he was grateful that even if they had taken everything that he had with him, it really wasn't much; and finally, he thanked God that he was the one who was robbed instead of being the thief. This man provides us with such a strong example of how every situation, as terrible as it might seem, always provides reasons for which we can be grateful. It is enough to be able to look at the situation with an open mind instead of complaining about it all the time.

If you still have doubts about the wonderful power of

gratitude, try contemplating how wonderful your own body is. You have a heart that beats without you having to ask it to. It keeps you alive from the day when it is formed in your mother´s womb until the moment when you leave this world. It is the same with every system in your body: they all work to keep you alive and thriving. You have an endless amount of air and the possibility of breathing without even thinking. You know that every inhalation is naturally followed by an exhalation. You have legs and feet that carry you from one place to the other and hands that can grasp food for your nourishment. Your eyes allow you to see the colors and landscapes, the smiles of children and of the ones you love. Your ears let you hear the music, while your mouth allows you to communicate your ideas. And if, for some reason, you have lost one of these faculties or they have diminished in health, you have the possibility to heal them or to discover new potentials in your body. There are people who run marathons without their legs and those who express themselves without words. Indeed, having a working body is a great reason to be thankful. Being alive is a great reason to be thankful.

As the practice of my gratitude progressed, and I kept studying the wellbeing that it offered my overall health, I was also filled with joy when I heard cases of other people who had also recovered by practicing daily appreciation for life. For example, have you heard about Team Hoyt? Rick Hoyt was born with a lack of oxygen flowing to his brain, which caused him to become quadriplegic and develop cerebral palsy. In 1977 Rick asked his father, Dick, if he would help him participate in a race to benefit a friend from school who had recently become paralyzed. Dick pushed Rick the entire five miles, and after participating in that race, Rick told his father that he wanted to participate in more race. Soon, they managed to complete triathlons, even though Dick didn't know how to swim or ride a bike, and he had to carry his son through the race. Their reputation solidified when the team successfully finished one of the most difficult athletic tests in the world: Ironman. I am sure that Rick was not focused on his paralysis during any of his races, but rather on gratitude for being able to be a part of this adventure that we call life.

Another benefit of gratitude is that it has helped me to focus on living in the present. Our minds often travel constantly from the past to the future. We are frequently remembering the experiences that we've already had and fixating on what we are going to do tomorrow. We rarely focus on enjoying and living fully in the present. For me, the past brought nostalgia and resentment, the future, anxiety and fear. When I started really appreciating my health, however, I found great value in my life and stopped worrying so much about the past or the future. I understood that, generally, the present always takes care of our true needs—that sometimes it doesn't provide what we think we need, but it always provides what is necessary. If you absorb everything that the present offers to you and manage to disconnect from both the past and the idea that you have of the future, you will realize that in this moment there are no risks or threats. When you feel fear, it's because you are projecting something in the future that you are usually comparing to a past experience.

There is an Eastern story that tells about the life of a warrior who had gone to prison. At night, the warrior couldn't sleep as he thought about the torture that he would receive in the morning. But the morning came and went without torture, and the warrior's uncertainty grew daily. One night, the warrior decided not to think about the next morning, and finally he slept. When he woke up, the doors of his cell were open and he just walked out. It is not simple to live in the present when you have so many pains from the past on your mind, but that is another wonder of gratitude, for with it also comes forgiveness towards yourself and others.

Resentment and bitterness are toxic to us. When we think about the circumstances or the people who have hurt us, we relive over and over the feelings that we had during that experience: fear, frustration, rage, etc., and we create a chain of negativity in our minds. Think of the instability that this can have on your health: high blood pressure, tachycardia, headaches, muscular tension, stomach pains... By forgiving, we detox, and the body balances. You are not punishing the one who hurt you when you don't forgive him; you are punishing yourself. When you appreciate your life, you also realize that it is pretty short and that you want to enjoy it to the utmost. You no longer want to carry on your shoulders the resentment, so you must start to let go of those thoughts that aren't useful to you. Every feeling of victimization then vanishes. I, for example, thought to myself, "Why waste my days with negative things that are no longer useful to me?" Negativity, with time, contributes to the deterioration of your mind and body, so it must be abandoned.

One of the first things that I noticed when I started forgiving was that I could feel compassion towards the same people who had hurt me. My anxiety and depression gradually disappeared while my immune system strengthened. It was as if suddenly that heavy load that I had carried for so many years had vanished, and I felt much lighter and yearned to do more things and just be happy. It's as if, miraculously, the thoughts of "nothing will turn out right" and "you are worthless" gave way to "give it a try." It really was like some inner voice told me, "I know that you can do a good job. You have the skills, and there is no reason why things should go wrong. Try, and you´ll see how well you do." The first time that I heard this echo within me, it sparked a significant change.

You don´t have to wait until you are sick like I was in order to start expressing gratitude. Remember that the bigger your gratitude, the more reasons your life will give you to be grateful. Start by being aware of simple things. For example, when you wash your hands, feel the water running through your fingers; notice its temperature, the scent of the soap, the smoothness of the bathroom sink. And as you are doing this, say to yourself, "now I am washing my hands. Now I am grabbing the soap. Now I´m smelling it. Now I´m turning the tap," and so on because every step that you take, no matter how small it may seem, is important when washing your hands. By doing this, you will one day surprise yourself by saying, "God, thank you for giving me hands. Thank you for the water. Thank you for the ability to clean my hands…" That way you will realize how wonderful a single moment truly is.

Many studies have been done on the power of gratitude, and the results are amazing, like the ones published by UCLA neuroscientist Dr. Alex Korb, who, in *Psychology Today*, says that, "gratitude, particularly if practiced regularly, can keep you healthier and happier. "[17] The study summarized an experiment conducted by two researchers from the United States, Emmons and McCullough, who examined two groups of people. The first group was asked to keep a daily diary that listed those things that they were grateful for. The other group was asked to record the reasons why they got angry and the reasons why they felt better than other people. The first group showed an increase in their attention, energy, enthusiasm, and determination, and even experienced the disappearance or reduction of some physical ailments compared to the second group.[18] Doctor Korb recommended in the same article to keep a "weekly gratitude journal" and mentions an experiment done in China where it was discovered that being grateful causes a decrease in anxiety and depression. Doctor Korb concluded by citing observations made by the National Institutes of Heath. This study found that a grateful attitude positively increases the activity of the hypothalamus, which is the

---

[17] Korb, Alex, "The Grateful Brain: The Neuroscience of Giving Thanks" Psychology Today, November 12, 2012. psychologytoday.com
https://www.psychologytoday.com/blog/prefrontal-nudity/201211/the-grateful-brain

[18] Emmons and McCullough 377

gland that controls functions like sleeping, eating, drinking, metabolic functioning, and stress levels. Similarly, in his book, <u>Thanks!: How the New Science of Gratitude Can Make You Happier</u>, psychologist Robert Emmons showed through many studies that gratitude positively influences the strengthening of the immune system, combats depression, reduces blood pressure, prevents heart disease, increases tolerance to pain, and encourages us to partake in physical activity and take care of our bodies.[19]

A study that I find particularly interesting is the one done jointly by the Psychology Department of George Mason University in Fairfax, Virginia, the University of Alabama, and the Western Veterans Administration Hospital of New York, in which it was discovered that "Dispositional gratitude predicted greater daily positive affect, percentage of pleasant days over the assessment period, daily intrinsically motivating activity, and daily self-esteem over and above effects attributable to PTSD severity and dispositional negative and positive affect in the PTSD group but not the non-PTSD group. Daily gratitude was uniquely associated with each dimension

---

[19] Robert Emmons, <u>Thanks!: How the New Science of Gratitude Can Make You Happier</u> (New York: Houghton Mifflin, 2007): 1-185

of daily well-being in both groups."[20]

I invite you to continue studying this topic for yourself. It was very interesting for me to corroborate the beneficial effects that the practice of gratitude brings at all levels. Below, I leave with you some very simple exercises that will help you start:

- When you wake up, just say thank you.

- When you go to bed, just say thank you.

- Once you´ve started to simply say thank you, you can begin adding thanks for those things, people, or situations that also inspire gratitude.

- Today, I am thankful because I can get out of bed.

- Today, I am thankful because I´m healthy

- Today, I am thankful because I have my health and food to eat (which many don´t have).

- Each day, you can keep on adding reasons why you express gratitude, and the less you think about it, the more reasons you will find because you´ll recognize

---

[20] Kashdan, T. Uswatte, G, et al., "Gratitude and Hedonic and Eudaimonic Well-Being in Vietnam War Veterans," <u>Journal of Behaviour Research and Therapy</u>, 44 (2006): 177-199

how the more you express thanks, the more you´ll
have to be grateful for.

Finally, I share with you the lyrics of a very famous
song, and one that I love a lot, by the Chilean singer
and composer Violeta Parra: "Thanks to life that has
given me so much. It has given me laughter and it has
given me tears…"

Cherish Your Body

Starting to care for and love my body was imperative to
my health and my ability to lead a full life. For me, this
part was the most significant of all because when I
really learned to take care of my body, I started to
respect, appreciate, love, and feel comfortable with
myself.

Have you ever traveled on a plane and paid attention to
the indications that the flight attendant gives before
takeoff? If the oxygen masks must be used, parents
should first put them on themselves before helping
their kids. Do you know the reason for this request? If
the parent loses consciousness, then the child will also
be defenseless. This scenario applies to life in general: it
isn't possible to take care of others if you don't take
care of yourself first. I understand that this is difficult
for people who grew up in conditions similar to mine,

where no one taught you the meaning of caring for yourself, since no one took care of them either. Maybe your parents didn't care about themselves because no one had shown them how to, since their parents were out of the house all day or working to support the family. Usually such behaviors become a cycle of bad habits that are passed down through generations. The main issue is that such traditions have been so deeply embedded in our minds that if we decide at any time to change and seize an opportunity to take care of ourselves a little, we feel guilty about it because we are convinced that that is a luxury that we don't deserve. And that same guilt could cause us to fall victim to resentment, depression, anger, stress, alcohol, eating disorders, toxic relationships, sleeping problems, and drug addiction.

For me, the feeling that "I am worthless" turned into "no one really cares about me," and so my needs had no true importance. This dragged me deeper into depression, rage, and anxiety, which were tools that I wrongly used to overcome the low self-esteem that plagued me. This is how we become victims of a vicious circle that we create for ourselves. I so distinctly remember when I used to wake up every morning in pain, with a sick body and tired, sad mind, but I still had to take care of everybody—everybody, that is, except myself. My family depended on me to cook for them and organize their activities. At work, my clients needed me to help them. But I felt like I had no one to depend on. Culturally, for me, this was a part of being a good mother, wife, and worker, and I accepted it as a normal behavior—a destiny that was thrust upon me and from which I couldn't escape. I felt a lot of resentment and sadness, and I even fantasized about divorcing the man I loved. I used to imagine that if we split up, we could share custody of the girls, and that way I would have some time, even a little, to dedicate to my healing and rest. These thoughts made me feel guilty while my self-esteem descended into the abyss, and I once gain became prisoner of a past that didn't allow me to move forward or to grow.

A guilty attitude can reach disastrous extremes, especially for mothers. And even if it is sometimes completely natural to feel overwhelmed or swamped, there are very few of us who take some time to relax, rest, and ease the mind. This constant sacrifice can trigger a serious and even mortal ailment, as in my case, or cause a person to commit suicide, destroy a family, or look for shelter in all kinds of physical, mental, and emotional addictions.

I remember an article that I read on CNN (May 6th, 2013), wherein the psychologist, Peggy Drexler, described the case of Brenda Heist, who, after leaving her small children at school, disappeared. Her family thought that something bad had happened to her or that she had died. After all, she was a wonderful mother, and no one could've imagined that Brenda simply abandoned her family that day. More than ten years went by before she turned herself in to the Florida state police, saying that she hadn't been kidnapped or injured, but that in the moment of abandonment, she felt stressed. Doctor Drexler writes, "Most mothers are familiar with the feeling -- for some it's more fleeting than for others -- of total exhaustion, frustration, a sense of being overwhelmed by duty and the responsibility of raising children. Maybe some indulge in a momentary fantasy of running away." [21]

It is also true, however, that the opposite can be true... if you allow yourself to do so. There are worse cases than Brenda's, but there is no need to arrive at the border of the abyss, ready to jump in. Instead, you can decide to change your attitude and start loving and respecting yourself. When I moved to Beverly Hills, I started socializing with mothers whose economic and social statuses were better than mine. I thought that

---

[21] Drexler, Peggy. "Why There Are More Walk-Away Moms" CNN, May 6, 2013, cnn.com,
http://www.cnn.com/2013/05/04/opinion/drexler-mothers-leaving/

these women had a deeper understanding than me, and I saw that they were fulfilled and sure of themselves— or at least that was how I perceived them. I also realized that they counted on family support, which I completely lacked. I remember hearing them comment that they took naps during the day if they felt tired; they went to the spa; they traveled alone with other friends and shared with their husbands, families, or nannies the upbringing of their children and the household's maintenance, thus allowing them to take a break when they needed it. To me, this seemed like a strange way of living, and a part of me even criticized these mothers for not taking complete charge of their families' needs. Sometimes I even felt anger and envy because they counted on the help that I so deeply yearned for. On the other hand, I admired them because these women were doing something that I wanted to experience, and they did it naturally and without any guilt. And their kids weren't poorly dressed, nor inadequately fed, nor ill-mannered… I thought to myself, "How am I going to take time for a nap with all of the responsibilities of the house, plus my duties of taking the girls to and from school and their activities, while also staying on top of my work and preparing food for my family?"

At times, I imagined that these mothers could afford those luxuries because, surely, they had grown up in families that had treated them with love, teaching them to respect their time, or because that same family was still with them, giving them support. Any thoughts of personal deficiency kept me in the role of victim and made me feel that I didn't deserve to be like these women who enjoyed basic wellbeing. However, an important element of my healing was understanding the importance that rest has in achieving optimum health. And I didn't need money to be able to rest! I just needed to face the truth that, just like the other mothers, I too had the right to take care of myself and rest when I needed it. In that sense, walking encouraged me immensely, for it cleared my mind and was very practical because instead of complaining that I had no one to take care of the girls for me, I took them with me, achieving a double benefit because their immune systems were fortified outdoors, and they had fun playing in nature.

Now, no matter how busy I am during the day, I always make sure to take even a little time to relax and clear my mind. Sometimes I sit somewhere in the house where I look out the window, without focusing on anything, and allow my eyes to get lost in the distance while simply resting. Other times, I let my thoughts focus on the positive aspects of a situation, in the lesson that it offers, the forgiveness that it requires, or the gratitude that it elicits, and then I continue my day with a much lighter and healthier attitude. This helps me enormously during stressful moments. I also like to set apart 10 or 15 minutes each day to dedicate to prayer. I know that I don't need to go to a church or temple; God is with me anywhere that I am in the present time. I usually pray when I go to bed and when I wake up, expressing my gratitude to God for the day that has passed or for the one that's about to begin, for the good and the bad because, as I said before, you learn from everything, and you grow as a result. The mere fact of praying and abandoning all to the hands of God greatly helps me to reduce my anxieties and insecurities. On other occasions, I go to the park and read a book that inspires me, or I call a friend and go to the theater or the movies. Meeting with my friends always give me energy, strengthens me, and helps me to laugh at things that I may be "taking too seriously."

Friends are very important. The first time that they introduced me to a Korean spa, I realized that the Korean culture is very clear on the effects of friendship and how to take care of oneself. I was fascinated by how women took care of one another, brushing their hair, giving each other foot massages, whispering to each other, taking naps together, enjoying the different hot and cold water fountains and saunas. I didn't understand what they were saying, but I could sense that they were talking to each other with love and understanding, without envy or criticism. Women of all ages, young and old, respected each other and provided support in a time of rest and recreation. I really enjoyed such an environment.

As I took care of myself, my physical, mental, and emotional health and my relationships with other people started to prosper because I felt happier, more positive, and more willing to live. So, I started making clearer and more beneficial decisions for my life, like when I stopped complaining about not having familial help and became a member of a group of mothers who provided a lot of mutual support. We gathered weekly with our children, organized game days, shared nannies, and even had a "mother´s only" night once a month. This helped me to find my own support group with other mothers, and I no longer felt so lonely. Maybe you could form your own group like this with your friends or join one that is already established.

Not feeling alone is very important, especially for the single mothers or fathers who sometimes don´t even have any financial assistance outside of their own work, which can make it almost impossible to take a break during the day. They work a lot, in their jobs and in their homes, and rarely have a moment for themselves. They also sleep very little because of stress about their children, and many times they even suffer discrimination in their jobs or get laid off for skipping work because of their children´s illnesses or needs. I felt great admiration for my own mother who, not long after arriving to this country, did everything by herself, including taking care of us and working full-time. Now I know that no one taught her to take care of herself, and maybe that is why I used to perceive that she rejected me. The mere fact that these women and men are alone should be motivation enough to start pampering themselves a little. What will happen to the children who only have one mother of father if the parent gets sick? You must take as much care of yourself as you take care of your kids. You don't have to wait for your life to be completely out of control to start taking care of yourself. You can start with a simple 10-minute nap. There are countries where taking a nap is a tradition. The word "siesta" comes from the Latin "sexta hora" (between 2:00 pm and 4:00 pm), which usually occurs after eating so that you can continue the day more relaxed, in a better mood, and with more vitality. Naptime can constitute either a brief rest of 10 minutes or up to an hour. Among its many benefits, we find that:

- It helps the mind to rest and clear.

- It relaxes and relieves tension.

- It helps maintain a healthy and natural beauty.

- It slows down premature aging caused by stress.

- It increases creative capacity, intuition, imagination, and, consequently, the ability to solve problems, for it relaxes and revitalizes the mind.

- It helps to maintain good psychic health because when you are rested, you remain in a positive mood.

- It reduces the risk of heart attack.

- It removes mental and physical fatigue, increasing your overall performance.

- It combats anxiety and stress.

- It offers a feeling of overall wellness.

It is a shame that in our culture, rest isn't given the importance that it deserves. However, the leaders of big companies, such as The Huffington Post and Google, "have created "nap rooms" for employees to grab a few z's in hopes of making them more productive at work."[22] In a study conducted by professor Matthew Walker and his team of researchers at UC Berkeley, they observed 39 adults and adolescents, then proved

---

[22] Stump, Scott. "Nap Rooms Encourage Sleeping on the Job Productivity" Today, 15 March, 2013, today.com http://www.today.com/money/nap-rooms-encourage-sleeping-job-boost-productivity-1C8881304

that those individuals who sleep up to 90 minutes during a nap have a greater capacity to learn. During the study, the subjects were given an exercise that stimulated the hippocampus, which is the region of the brain associated with memory. After two hours, one part of the group went to sleep while the other part stayed awake. Once the group was reassembled, another learning test was administered, which corroborated that the ones who had rested demonstrated better results than those who stayed awake.[23] If you are wondering if there is a duration that maximizes the results, I can tell you that in 1995, NASA conducted a study on napping and concluded that, "a 26-minute nap would improve performance by 34% and alertness by 54%."[24]

Taking care of myself not only helped me to improve my health but also to eliminate stresses, which, as we all know, causes imbalances and ailments in the body. I have no doubt that my anxieties caused me a lot of stress, which in time led to my problems with my immune system. That is why I never tire of reminding

[23] Walker, Matthew., Mander, Byce., et al., "Wake Deterioration and Sleep Restoration of Human Learning." Current Biology 21 (2011): 183-184

[24] Geoghegan, Tom. "Who, What, Why: How Long Is the Ideal Nap?" *BBC News*. BBC, 29 Apr. 2011.

my clients about the importance of not letting stress overtake their lives. Stress is a load of tension that arises as a reaction of the body, mind, or emotions to a demand, challenge, or overall situation. It is silent, and we often aren't aware of how stressed we are. In a few cases, stress can be positive, like in moments when it helps us to escape imminent danger, but usually stress is harmful.

Currently, especially in big cities around the world, individuals and families are forced to deal with long commutes to work or school, a significant increase in work hours, and economical and social uncertainty. Such circumstances provoke more tension in our lives and increase our daily stress. Unfortunately, we live in a society that increasingly depends on our level of productivity. This doesn't leave us time to dedicate to ourselves, our significant others, or families or friends. In metropolitan areas, people may also live quite isolated lives, and when loneliness becomes a habit, it turns dangerous for our health and can lead us back to a vicious cycle of low self-esteem, eating disorders, depression, and addictions. Again, parents and single mothers, especially those who lack familial or communal support, are an easy target for daily stress and risk it becoming a chronic condition. According to statistics, "110 million people die every year as a direct result of stress. That is 7 people every 2 seconds!" [25]

Stress has been associated with:

- Obesity/Eating Disorders.

- Hair loss.

- Anxiety and depression.

- Sexual problems (low libido, impotence).

- Irregular menstruation and pre-menstrual syndrome.

- Infertility.

- Problems with the skin.

- Stomach diseases.

- Insomnia.

- Heart disease (According to Columbia University Medical Center, "general stress is related to heart health. In comparison with traditional cardiovascular

---

[25] "7 People Die From Stress Every 2 Seconds." Richmond Hypnosis Center 12 April, 2013 richmondhypnosiscenter.com http://richmondhypnosiscenter.com/2013/04/12/sample-post-two/

risk factors, high stress provides … the equivalent of … smoking five more cigarettes per day."**26**).

- Hypertension.

- Immune system disorders.

- Arthritis.

- Inflammation.

- Constipation.

- Divorce.

During my investigations about the influence of stress on my health, I found some studies that were of great interest to me. For example, according to the American Psychological Association, the family life of a single father/mother, even if it is fairly common, can be quite stressful for both the adult and the child. Members of the family have the idealized hope that they can work as a two-parent family and then feel that something is wrong when this expectation is not met. The single

---

[26] "Perceived Stress May Predict Future Risk of Coronary Heart Disease" Columbia University Medical Center, December, 2012. www.newsroom.cumc.columbia.edu http://newsroom.cumc.columbia.edu/blog/2012/12/17/perceived-stress-may-predict-future-risk-of-coronary-heart-disease/

father/mother may feel overwhelmed by the responsibility of having to juggle raising the kids, keeping his/her job, paying the bills, and maintaining the household. Generally, finances and family resources are drastically reduced after the parents' separations.[27] Furthermore, a group of scientists at the Clinical Institute of Laboratory Medicine at the MedUni Vienna, under the guidance of Martin Bilban, proved that there is a close link between stress and obesity: "When someone is suffering from raised stress levels, increased amounts of glucocorticoids are secreted. These play a part in becoming overweight. Up until now it has not been clear why fat tissue is formed primarily in the belly as abdominal or visceral fat... [But] changes in the formation of LMO3 play an important role in the re-distribution of the fat tissue in the direction of belly fat – these changes are triggered by the higher glucocorticoid level and by the 11β-HSD1 enzyme... The study's authors were thus able to demonstrate that LMO3- and 11β- HSD1-levels in the belly fat of obese patients are closely correlated. Furthermore, both also promote the formation of fat cells. In this, LMO3 has a stimulating effect at molecular level on PPARγ, the key gene in the

---

[27] "Parenting: Being Supermom Stressing You Out." American Psychological Association, May 2011. apa.org
http://www.apa.org/helpcenter/supermom.aspx

formation of fat."[28]

Dr. Cesáreo Fernández Alonso from the Emergency Service and Short Stay Unit of the San Carlos Clinical Hospital in Madrid stated that, "stress is considered the trigger or shutter of numerous cardiovascular diseases in susceptible individuals: brain ischemia (stroke) and myocardial diseases (angina pectoris, symptomatic or asymptomatic infarction). It is also associated with arterial hypertension and malignant arrhythmias. At the same time, it powers the rest of the factors in cardiovascular risk. There is clear evidence of the influence of the endocrine cycles on cardiovascular disease."[29]

Stress has also been related to intestinal inflammatory diseases, like ulcerative colitis and Crohn's disease, and associated with several symptoms, like diarrhea and abdominal pain. According to best-selling author and

---

[28] Bilban, Martin., "Human but not Mouse Adipogenesis is Critically Dependent on LMO3." Journal of Cell Metabolism, 18 (2013): 62-74

[29] Fernando, Cesareo. "El Estrés en las Enfermedades Cardiovasculares." Libro de la Salud Cardiovascular del Hospital Clínico San Carlos y la Fundación BBVA (2009) Capítulo 66, 583-590
http://www.fbbva.es/TLFU/microsites/salud_cardio/mult/fbbva_libroCorazon.pdf

recognized professional, Doctor Joseph Mercola:

"The stress response causes a number of detrimental events in your gut, including:

- Decreased nutrient absorption.

- Decreased oxygenation to your gut.

- As much as four times less blood flow to your digestive system, which leads to decreased metabolism.

- Decreased enzymatic output in your gut as much as 20,000-fold!"[30]

Likewise, the *Journal of Physiology and Pharmacology* noted that, "Stress, which is defined as an acute threat to homeostasis, shows both short- and long-term effects on the functions of the gastrointestinal tract."[31]

The main effects that stress has on intestinal physiology include:

---

[30] Dr. Mercola. How Stress Makes You Sick. Dec. 17, 2015. mercola.com https://goo.gl/38QHUW
[31] Konturek, PC., Brzozowski, T., Konturek, SJ. Stress and the Hut: Pathophysiology, Clinical Consequences, Diagnostic Approach and Treatment Options. Journal of Physiology and Pharmacology. 69 (2011) 591-599

- Alterations in the gastrointestinal motility.

- Increase in the visceral perception.

- Changes in gastrointestinal secretion.

- Negative effects on the regenerative capacity of the gastrointestinal mucus and the blood flow of the mucus.

- Negative effects on the intestinal microflora.

Doctor Mercola explains that stress goes hand-in-hand with the following inflammatory diseases: Multiple Sclerosis, Lupus, Renal Problems, Chronic Fatigue Syndrome, type-1 Diabetes, Urinary Diseases, Fibromyalgia, Rheumatoid Arthritis, Ulcerative Colitis, Allergies, Myalgic Encephalomyelitis, Osteoarthritis, Chronic Skin Diseases, and Degenerative Diseases. As you can see, the sources of stress are endless, and they all contribute to the adverse effects that stress has on our health.

Unfortunately, stress may be unavoidable, but the good news is that it can be controlled. To reduce stress, I had to identify the root of what was causing me to experience anxiety and fear. One exercise that helped me a lot was recording in a notebook the situations and people who caused me more stress, which helped me to start recognizing its symptoms. I must point out here that the symptomatology of stress may be different for each person. In my case, it manifested itself as anxiety, immune system problems, depression, and stomach aches. Reading my notes cleared my mind and motivated me to take care of myself because the more I did it, the easier it was for me to face stressful situations or identify how to completely avoid them. Only you know what causes you anxiety, fear, and, consequentially, stress. Sometimes it can be something so normal in our lives that may go unnoticed, but when you take the time to write it, you start to recognize the sources of your stress, and your way of dealing it will change for the better.

In my private practice, I see numerous clients whose main source of stress is constant work or loneliness. These people usually overload themselves with work and submit themselves to rigorous agendas in order avoid arriving home to an empty house or spending time by themselves. In this way, they lock themselves up in an apparatus that doesn't allow them to have a significant other, or meet up with a group of friends or those who may become friends because they are bogged down by the massive load of self imposed activities that they have clung to. On the other hand, out of fear of being alone, they allow themselves to be abused or taken advantage of. Here I want to remind you once again that when you start taking care of yourself, you also start giving yourself the value that you deserve, and this kind of victimization stops happening to you.

I also have clients who, even if they are surrounded by family, struggle with the burden of stress because family can be dysfunctional, abusive, or overprotective. And if they want to free themselves from the family burden, they feel guilty because they experience the social pressure that often plagues us when we decide to pull away from a close family member because those on the outside of the situation don´t see how much damage is being done to us by the family member in question. I also have clients who feel guilty because they think that they are "the ones who are wrong," or "the ones who are bad," when it is obvious that the fault resides in the other individual. There are times when it is very hard to accept the truth, as often happens to those who have been abused by their parents. For these people, living every day in an unhappy situation triggers chronic stress, which manifests itself with even more intensity during Christmas or family celebrations, especially when they see commercials that show happy, united families. Such visuals remind them of the contradiction of their own lives compared to what they see in the advertisements. Stress is so embedded that many times they don't realize that these commercials aren't an accurate reflection of real life and that many families aren't as happy as the ads make them look.

I should be clear: it is not my intention to suggest you that you pull away from your family. I am aware that there is no perfect family, but I simply advise you to be aware in case you are suffering from unhealthy family mechanisms, and that you try to avoid getting into any unhealthy situations. I know that there are many cases in which they can't be avoided, and then it is preferable to be prepared to face them in the most relaxed way possible. For example, if you find yourself at a family Christmas dinner and your sister or your parents start criticizing you in some way, instead of receiving their harsh words with negativity or starting a heated discussion, try building a bridge between you and them rather than a barrier. Thank them for the suggestions and tell them that you are going to think about it, then subtly change the topic of conversation. Unfortunately, there are times when you have tried it all and nothing works. It is then necessary to get away from all of the negative people in our lives and remove ourselves from their dramas, even if they are a part of our family. A "well-meaning" friend may criticize you and treat you badly, simply because he or she wants you to behave in a specific way that will benefit him or her. Many times, parents engage in this unhealthy behavior, and it causes their children a lot of stress. I have personally had to learn to say no without feeling guilty, and it wasn't an easy task, but with practice and the willingness to love to myself, I achieved it. I am confident that you can too.

Another example that I often see in my consultations is that of families who have placed a lot of expectations upon a person, thus creating too much pressure for them to "shine" or "be successful in life." It may happen that these individuals don't meet the expectations, which are often ridiculous and unachievable, and then they suffer from depression under the accusing gaze of their relatives who regularly remind them that they "have failed." Many parents do this with their children when they try to live their own unreached dreams through their children without care about whether their children share these goals. I know that as parents, we all want what is best for our children, but sometimes it is easy to mix our own dreams and desires in with the lives of our children. Not long ago, I had a client who had this problem with her parents, and we immediately began working on reminding her that it is her life— the only one she´s got to live— and not her parents', sibling´s, or grandparents'. We all know, in the bottom of our hearts, what our life goals and dreams are. By chasing them, we find self-realization.

Many times we make the mistake of getting angry or taking it out on ourselves when we can´t say no, but we gain nothing by treating ourselves badly. On the contrary, we cause more stress to our systems when we do so. Stay positive, try to modify the negative thoughts that haunt you, and be sure to solve the problem or look for help to solve it when it arises. Usually when I take care of my problems instead of worrying about them, I feel great relief. Knowing that I am searching for a solution gets me out of the role of victim and empowers me.

Another very important aspect when you decide to take care of yourself, and that generally goes unnoticed, resides in the importance of sleeping at least seven or eight hours each night. On occasion, this may be quite a challenge. I struggled with this due to my anxieties and my illnesses; I couldn't sleep because of the pain, and I was tired all day, as I struggled to focus and maintain a positive mood. When you don't sleep well, you usually resort to foods and substances that cause a temporary increase of energy, like sweets, caffeinated drinks, and complex carbohydrates. What your body is actually asking for is rest, not caffeine and sugar. In Los Angeles, where I currently live, there is a coffee shop on practically every corner of the city. This promotes the concept of constantly drinking caffeine, to such a degree that it becomes a lifestyle. Some of my clients have contacted me because they have difficulty losing weight since they don't sleep enough and resort to "eating all the time" to feel more vitality. But none of this replaces the benefits of sleeping well; on the contrary, many times my clients get sick due to the lack of rest and excessive intake of sugar foods that keep them "awake" during the day.

There are numerous studies that indicate a correlation between obesity and lack of sleep, and many of these also mention the development of diabetes as a result. Investigations indicate that this could be the result of an altered glucose metabolism because of the lack of sleep and the weight gain, in combination with the fact that you expend less energy and eat more when you are exhausted, leaving fewer possibilities of undertaking physical activity.

Thus, people get fat and find themselves locked in a vicious cycle. It is very important that if you are trying to lose weight, you focus on the kind of relationship that you have with sleep because by simply changing this one aspect of your life, your weight may return to normal. So, if you feel that you are not sleeping enough, try modifying your lifestyle, and you'll soon feel much better—rested, refreshed, energetic.

Sleeping for at least seven or eight hours can bring you

the following benefits:

- Increases immunity.

- Weight loss.

- Increases mental wellbeing.

- Diabetes prevention.

- Increases sexual desire.

- Heart disease prevention.

- Increases fertility.

The Institute of Sleep Medicine in Valencia, Spain, says that in general, what happens while we sleep isn't known with scientific accuracy, but what we do know it that each sleep phase is involved in a different task. During deep sleep, there is a physical restoration, and during REM sleep there is a cognitive function restoration (processes of learning, memory, and concentration). In this way, what we have learned during the day reaffirms itself. In popular culture, we find phrases and sayings that adhere to this concept, like "slept lesson, learnt lesson," or "talk it over with your pillow." Currently, there are many factors that demonstrate how adequate sleep matters. Work and school performance, the length of the healing process, the occurrences of exhaustion-based accidents, and so much more illustrate how important sleep is to our wellbeing. Modern life demands a permanent learning process, attention, concentration, monitoring, and cognitive functions, like driving, control, and observation, all of which a good night's sleep facilitates. Therefore, inadequate sleep has important social and medical consequences that affect people of all ages and social statuses equally.[32]

I would like to share with you some very simple exercises that help me in the process of taking care of myself. With time and practice, you'll find you own method. For now, the following can give you an idea of how to start:

- I express my needs and feelings (even if I initially felt guilty, I did it anyway).

- I don't compare myself with others (each one of us is important in this universe, and no one has more value than another. Besides, all people have problems, to a greater or lesser extent).

---

[32] "La Importancia de Dormir Bien." Instituto de Medicina del Sueño, http://www.dormirbien.info/trastornos-del-sueno/la-importancia-de-dormir-bien/

- I find the time to enjoy simple things in life (a walk in the woods, a moment in the park, or a break during the day).

- I socialize with people who appreciate me as I am, support me, share my ideas and my dreams, and help me get by. When we don't agree, we have the freedom to express our feelings and opinions freely, without guilt or manipulations.

- I don't complain anymore, but rather seize the opportunities of growth that life offers to me.

- I dedicate time to relaxation and my personal moments.

- I know how to say "no" and "enough."

- I do work that I enjoy.

- I exercise at least three times per week.

- I make smart choices with my diet.

- I try to help others as often as I can (service to others is service to ourselves)

- I identify, hear, and follow the advice of my "inner voice."

- I give no importance to "what others might say" and understand how negative criticism of others might adversely affect my health.

By learning to take care of myself, I inevitably started loving my body. It's something that comes naturally— one thing follows the next because the more you take care of your body, the more you love it, since you realize how amazing it is. With love, you learn to listen to your body and accept it as it is, to understand it and cherish it.

There are people who sometimes look at me as if I am crazy when I tell them that my body can let me know when I am tired, sick, or stressed. Nowadays, unfortunately, we live such a busy life that ignoring messages from the body is the norm. And sometimes when we do finally listen to them, it is too late. For example, a simple cold or headache is the way that your body has of saying that it feels tired, and it is time to rest. So, instead of taking a couple of pills and continuing with your routine, it would be a better choice to stay home and give your body some peace, especially considering that sometimes one day of rest is enough to return to full health. Otherwise, you risk having temporary relief from the pills but coming down with something stronger a few days later, perhaps a migraine or the flu, because you didn't take the time to heal yourself.

I remember a saying that I heard once that had quite an impact on me: "the only disease that endures is ignorance." Once I understood that, I became aware of the things that aided or derailed my wellbeing. I remember the moment when I first realized this: one day, I noticed that I was losing my hair. Anguished, I call my rheumatologist, who explained to me that hair loss is a side effect of the medicine that I was taking for the pain and swelling, and that it is normal. His answer shocked and worried me because now I had to add hair loss to my daily suffering. So, I decided to read the side effects of the medication that I was taking. To my horror, I realized that what was supposed to help me could simultaneously cause liver problems, blood anomalies (which I was already suffering from!), and cancer, among other things. Despite my anguish, I kept reading the side effects of the other medication that I was taking, and I learned that the medicine prescribed by my gastroenterologist could cause irreparable damage to my liver and kidneys, cancer, convulsions, and fatal infections (I already had infections all the time!), among other things. The medicine prescribed by the hematologist could cause diarrhea, vomiting, constipation, muscle aches, chronic fatigue, body and bones aches, etc. The antibiotics that my primary care physician constantly gave me – as I mentioned, my immune system was shot, and I suffered from infections regularly – could cause yeast infections, intestinal, liver, and stomach problems, among other issues. To treat the yeast infection, the gynecologist ordered me medicine that could cause renal problems, stomach aches, and other disorders in my body. Moreover, I also took a pill to calm the anxiety that my disease and all of my medications' side effects caused me.

Once you get into the circle, it is very difficult to get out because the pills do offer temporary relief of your ailments. I used to have variety of different diagnoses with different doctors. Each one of them prescribed me a different medicine without knowing how they interacted with my other medications. To this stress, I had to add that during my consultations, I felt rushed: no doctor seemed to have enough time to listen to my problems and study my particular case. The only things that they did during my appointment were order exams and analyses and prescribe medicine without worrying about how it was all affecting me. I think that this contributes, in many cases, to addictions to prescription drugs.

From my experience, I know that my case is not at all unique. Unfortunately, the culture in which we live – especially Western culture— doesn't have "the time" to dedicate to complete healing. Nowadays, everything must be immediate and with quick gratification. But this doesn't work for our bodies. The mindset that has been created in recent years that idolizes pills as an absolute solution keeps you away from the knowledge that, in reality, it is the wrong thoughts and actions that lead you to your unhappiness and unhealthiness. In fact, there are more people every day who suffer from chronic ailments. On a daily basis, I see clients who take medication and have no idea how it affects their bodies and pushes them away from their healing. I remember one client who took medicine for depression because she felt fat and couldn't lose weight. She felt that it was impossible for her to stop eating in excess. When I read the side effects of the medication, I realized that among them were increases in appetite and anxiety. Of course, in some cases depression can increase or decrease appetite, but in the case of my client, she got worse because of the medicine that she was taking to "heal." She had no idea about this side effect that was keeping her in a cycle of sadness and overeating!

To heal requires patience. There are many of us who have chosen the path of self-healing and have gone through this experience, and that is why we are aware that the process doesn't happen overnight. What gives us strength to continue on is the will and the desire to emerge from the swamp of unhappiness and discomfort into the sensation of light and complete wellbeing. That being said, I want to make clear that it is not my intention to criticize doctors or Western medicine that has been proven to be beneficial and has saved lives on countless occasions. I also don't want to suggest that you stop taking your medication. I just want to educate you about the way that certain things may be negatively affecting your body and help you to explore other possibilities that you can use alongside the treatment that you think is best for you. Thanks to my experience, I have been able to take control of my life and look for help. I was thirty years old at the time, and it was unbearable for me to think that I was going to live like this for the rest of my days—a life filled with pain and suffering, wherein if the disease didn't kill me, medicine would. If I was going to get better, I couldn't be codependent on medicine that on the one hand helped me, but on the other hand annihilated me. My healing had to be complete.

As I mentioned earlier, the desperation of not finding a solution through traditional means inspired me to look for the help of a holistic healer who taught me to be much more attentive to the kind of food that I consumed because everything that you put in your body, whether it's medicine, food, or thoughts, affects you physically and mentally. According to the healer, my body suffered from chronic inflammation— which caused the decrease in white blood cells, the chronic infections, the maladies in my intestines, the pain, etc.—due to my anxiety and all of the chemicals and artificial ingredients of the processed and refined products that I ate. This was the first time that I had heard the words "chronic inflammation," and I had never imagined that an inflamed body could cause so much damage.

For me, inflammation in the body was the result of transitory pain related to an accident, not physical or emotional problems. I also was very surprised when he associated my eating habits with my health problems and gave me the understanding that if I kept fueling myself with junk food and processed meals, I wasn't going to get better. Admittedly, at first, I didn't believe him— after all, I had grown up eating anything I wanted and had never been sick. I also naively thought that problems with food, such as allergies, diseases, and obesity, were things that only wealthy people suffered from. Poor people who didn't know where their next meal was coming from, who ate what they could, did not care about allergies or diseases. To be honest, I had never heard that a person could be allergic to certain foods until I migrated to the United States. Besides, I loved American food, and it was hard for me to associate it with damage to my health. But I couldn't stand the physical pain that, according to him, these foods and artificial chemicals were causing me. Back then, I remembered a saying that said that, "the scars that you can't see are the hardest to heal," and that is why I decided to take control of my health, including any and everything that could harm my mind and body. To do so, I had to accept that my body is my temple, and I must love it just the way it is, with all of its "weaknesses and strengths." So, I began the task of learning about the foods that could heal me, the ones that harmed me, and the way that my body processed them upon consumption.

The first thing that I did was learn everything about inflammation, especially which foods and chemicals caused it in my body, so that I could start eliminating them from my diet and thus start the process of healing. Inflammation (from Latin inflammare, which means light fire) is a way in which the immune system responds to invaders, such as virus and bacteria. In this process, different kinds of white blood cells travel through the bloodstream to the place of infection, and once there, they request more white blood cells. Once the inflammation or threat disappears, the inflammation dissipates. In this case, the inflammation helps the process of healing because it generally comes with an increase in body temperature. Traditional medicine tends to avoid this by, for example, "lowering the fever," but really, the mechanisms that eliminate the toxins in the body accelerate when the body temperature arises. This is a beneficial procedure, even if we don't realize it at the time. Let´s be clear, however, that if the fever gets to a dangerous level, of course it is necessary to control it.

Problems appear when the body becomes inflamed as a result of different irritants, such as junk food, stress, lack of sleep, anxiety, and depression, because in these situations your body thinks it has to "detox" from this strange elements, and it then continues its own treatment. In other words, the inflammation never goes away, thus becoming what we call "chronic inflammation." This is very difficult to treat because you generally don't realize that you are suffering from it until your health starts failing. When the inflammation begins travelling through your blood stream without healing, it produces harmful effects all over the body.

Many of the studies that I read showed, time and again, that chronic inflammation is the root of numerous diseases, including those where it is obvious, like rheumatoid arthritis and obesity, and those where it isn't obvious, like Alzheimer's, cancer, arteriosclerosis, diabetes, chronic fatigue, and autoimmune disorders. For example, in a study conducted at the Brigham and Women's Hospital in Boston, 28,000 women were examined during a period of eight years, and it was discovered that "inflammation in blood vessels is twice as likely as high cholesterol to lead to heart disease... The study showed that women with high levels of CRP [which is produced by the body when it's fighting injury and infection] were twice as likely as those with high cholesterol to die from heart attacks and strokes. It also showed about half of heart attacks and strokes occurred in those with seemingly safe levels of cholesterol. "[33] CRP (for C Reactive Protein) is a substance associated with the inflammatory state that is produced by the liver and by some cells in the immune system. New studies indicate that the presence of high levels of this substance may be as useful (if not more so) than the levels of cholesterol in determining the probability of someone suffering a heart attack or a stroke.

Another article that I found very interesting was published by the Sapienza University of Rome, Italy. It mentioned practically every symptom that I had when it cited evidence, "linking alterations in the inflammatory system to Major Depression, including the presence of elevated levels of pro-inflammatory cytokines, together with other mediators of inflammation... Indeed,

---

[33] Morales, Tatiana., "Inflammation Linked to Heart Illness," CBSNews, Nov. 14, 2002, cbsnews.com, http://www.cbsnews.com/news/inflammation-linked-to-heart-ills/

systemic infections, cancer or autoimmune diseases, as well as stressful life events, are characterized by an activation of the peripheral immune system, which is part of the required response of the body to cope with the adverse condition. However, when the activation of the immune system is prolonged, for example because of a persistence of the adverse event, cytokines and other immune modulators can access the brain and affect different brain systems that play a role in enhancing vulnerability to depressive disorders."[34]

What I found didn't fail to amaze me, even as I read the same results over and over again. Certain behaviors were devastating for the body, especially consumption of certain foods that I myself consumed daily and which caused the decrease of white blood cells, inflammation in the body, and rheumatoid arthritis. Even if the modern cure to reduce inflammation consists of taking medicines, I can assure you that for me, such a line of treatment was in vain, and my issues were permanently solved when I changed my diet and lifestyle. The more I learned about healthy food, the

---

[34] Cattaneo, Annamaria., Macchi, Flavia., et al., "Inflammation and Neuronal Plasticity: A Link Between Childhood Trauma and Depression Pathogenesis," Journal of Frontiers in Cellular Neuroscience 9 (2015): Article 40.
https://www.ncbi.nlm.nih.gov/pmc/articles/PMC4379909/

more I remembered how I had eaten while growing up in La Romana. Even if food was scarce, back then we didn't have processed food riddled with pesticides, artificial additives, and genetically modified organisms. Food was always homemade, and for economic reasons, we never ate out. I also ate more fresh fruit and vegetables, and the meat that I consumed came from animals raised on farms, in their natural environments and without hormones. At that time, the difficult life that I had and the need to do "everything fast" caused me to forget the essential rules that my mother and grandmother used to apply at the time of eating. Now, years later, I started changing my diet to align more with the eating style that I had during my childhood.

As I ate fresher food, my health began to improve. Little by little, my white blood cells started increasing while infections decreased. I couldn't believe that the cure for my physical pain was the nourishment that I gave my body! As my health kept improving, the progress gave me more reasons to keep on with my personal research. I became practically obsessed with everything related to nutrition, and I developed such a massive passion for the topic that once I was completely healed, I decided to go back to school and study nutrition with the goal of educating myself more and also being able to help others, who, just like me, didn't have (and still don't) the knowledge that the key to healing their maladies could be sitting on the dinner plate in front of them

At this point, I want to mention that I am aware that none of us are the same—that each body reacts differently and that what helped me perhaps won't be the same for you, just like what negatively affected me won't necessarily hurt you. That is why I believe that when you love your body, you start paying attention to it and start knowing what you need, including which foods make you feel better and which are toxic for your body.

Your body will thank you

"If you don't care for your body, where are you thinking of living?" – Unknown author.

Unfortunately, many people have no idea how food can affect their bodies. That is why I would like to share with you, in more detail, some of the knowledge about the unhealthy food that caused so much damage to my wellbeing, and also the healthy ones that have helped me to strengthen my immune system and my body in general. I hope that this information not only helps you and broadens your understanding of this topic, but also empowers you to improve your health.

Most of processed foods that I ate were, for the most part, refined, filled with sugar, fat, artificial flavors, and colors, and made with genetically modified ingredients (GMO) – and I had no idea! My first step was the elimination of processed and refined foods— those foods that, by the magic of modern technology, you heat up for a few minutes and are ready to eat, emerging from the mystical microwave steaming and full of flavor. This kind of food only fills your stomach, because when it is processed, it loses the fiber, water, minerals, and vitamins that are necessary for your body to be healthy, happy, and energetic.

One of the greatest dangers of processed food is that it causes addiction. The ingredients are designed to make us eat more because after we consume them, we feel a pleasant sensation thanks to the additives. Besides, since these meals don't have any kind of nutritional value, we eat more than necessary, as the body continues to think that it is "starving" because it isn't getting the nutrition that it needs. From this point, it is a short step into obesity and illness.

On the list of refined and processed foods that I had to remove from my diet were precooked foods like sausages and cold cuts, salami, bacon, pizza, chicken nuggets, chocolate (to be clear, raw, organic, and unrefined chocolate is very good for the health), french fries, and food made with white flour, like bread, pasta, and cookies. I also gradually eliminated white rice. In addition, I stopped eating at fast food restaurants like McDonald´s (one of my favorites, especially because my first job when I arrived in the U.S. was at a McDonald´s), Burger King, Kentucky Fried Chicken, Wendy´s, Taco Bell, In-N-Out, and Dunkin´ Donuts, among others. I don't mean to bash any of these restaurants, but rather to clarify that the speed and convenience with which meals are prepared at such restaurants are accompanied by a high price paid with our health because their main components are sugar, salt, hydrogenated oils (trans fats), artificial additives, and coloring. All of these ingredients are addictive, make us eat more, and have been associated with depression, cancer, emotional diseases, and immune imbalances. Doctor Robert Lustig from the Endocrine Department at the University of California, San Francisco, explains that processed carbohydrates can affect brain chemistry in the same way that drugs like cocaine do.35 In other research done at the Child´s Hospital in Boston, under the supervision of David Ludwig, a study indicated that, " substance abuse and food with a high glycaemic index - such as white bread and potatoes - may trigger the same brain mechanism tied to addiction"[35]–to the point that "brain activity [is]

---

[35] "Sugar: The Bitter Truth." University of California Television,

similar to heroin users after eating certain processed foods."[36] While the brain chemistry is a convincing fact, perhaps the more visible consequences of consuming a diet of processed and refined foods are obesity and a weakened immune system. What happens to the body after eating these meals is that that without having the vitamins, minerals, and nutrients, we do not "feel full," and so we continue to be hungry; even if you eat more of this food to try to satiate your hunger, in time, the body becomes weak

Watch the salt!

Another ingredient that, like refined sugar and high fructose corn syrup, causes disease is refined table salt. The use of salt stimulates the intake of food because it enhances its flavor and therefore makes it more appealing. Salt is used as a meat preservative (in sausages, hams, salami), with fish (like cured cod,

---

Julio 27, 2009. http://uctv.tv/shows/Sugar-The-Bitter-Truth-16717
David S. Ludwig., Dorota B. Polack., and Cara B. Ebbeling., "Childhood Obesity: Public-Health Crisis, Common Sense Cure," The Lancet, 360 (2002): 473-482
[36] Collis, Helen. "Food Really Is Addictive: Study Finds Brain Activity Similar to Heroin Users after Eating Certain Processed Foods." *Daily Mail Online*. Associated Newspapers, 27 June 2013.

herring, sardines), and as a seasoning. Unfortunately, not all salt is created equal. I realized this when I learned that salt could also be the cause of many of my physical ailments. Refined salt has had its minerals removed, and has been bleached and exposed to many chemicals that are poisonous to the body. This kind of salt is among the causes of many diseases like rheumatism, arthritis, high blood pressure, heart disease, diabetes, and renal conditions.

In its natural state, unrefined salt is rich in minerals and trace elements (calcium, magnesium chloride, potassium, iodine, and manganese), while the main component of table or refined salt is sodium chloride, which is highly concentrated, denatured and toxic for the body, as it cannot absorb naturally. In a study published by the New England Journal of Medicine, researchers specified that, "1.65 million deaths from cardiovascular causes… worldwide in 2010 were attributable to sodium consumption above the reference level. Of these deaths, 687,000 (41.7%) were due to coronary heart disease, 685,000 (41.6%) were due to stroke, and 276,000 (16.7%) were due to other cardiovascular disease."[37] According to the Dietary

---

[37] Dariush, Mozaffarian., Saman, Fahimi., Gitanjali, Singh., et al., "Global Sodium Consumption and Death from Cardiovascular Causes." The New England Journal of Medicine,

Guidelines for Americans, it is "recommend that Americans consume less than 2,300 milligrams (mg) of sodium per day as part of a healthy eating pattern…. Based on these guidelines, the vast majority of adults eat more sodium than they should—an average of more than 3,400 mg each day"[38] The American Heart Association suggests an intake of 1.500 grams daily, especially for those who suffer from the heart, diabetes, and high blood pressure. It also mentions that, "About 90% of Americans' sodium intake comes from sodium chloride (or table salt). More than 75 percent of the sodium Americans eat comes from some processed, prepackaged and restaurant foods – not from the salt shaker."[39]

It is very easy to consume a lot of salt in precooked or processed meals because most of them contain high percentages of salt, much more so that the recommended daily serving. For example, I used to love hot dogs, and while I was informing myself on this

---

371 (2014): 624-634

[38] "Get the Facts: Sodium and the Dietary Guidelines," Center for Disease Control and Prevention, April 4th, 2016, https://www.cdc.gov/salt/pdfs/Sodium_Dietary_Guidelines.pdf
[39] "Sodium and Your Health," American Heart Association, heart.org
https://sodiumbreakup.heart.org/sodium_and_your_health

subject, I decided to look into their sodium content. I was amazed when I realized that a single hot dog had 790 milligrams of salt— that is without counting the french fries that often accompany it, which have almost 300 milligrams for every ten fries! This combination alone was half of the daily amount that is recommended by American health institutions. Here I leave you an idea of how much sodium there is in varying spoon sizes of salt, according to the American Heart Association:

- ¼ teaspoon of salt = 575 mg of sodium

- ½ teaspoon of salt = 1,150 mg of sodium

- ¾ teaspoon of salt = 1,725 mg of sodium

- 1 teaspoon of salt = 2,300 mg of sodium

In contrast to table salt and additives in processed foods, natural salts like Himalayan pink salt, a favorite among holistic and health-conscious chefs, and sea salt are very beneficial for the body. Himalayan salt, for example, has been used for over 250 million years and is the purest kind of salt that there is on our planet, as it is free from all contamination. Its benefits include the regulation of water in our bodies, the prevention of muscle cramps, the regulation of sleep, the maintenance of a healthy libido, the prevention of varicose veins in the legs, and the stabilizing of irregular heartbeats, among other things. Unrefined sea salt, obtained through sea water evaporation, is good for digestion, regulates PH levels in the body (creating a balance between acidity and alkalinity), helps to keep muscles in shape, and balances blood pressure.

I want to add that a high intake of sodium – even from natural salt sources -- is not good for our health. What's important is knowing that refined salt doesn't add anything to our bodies' nutrition, while natural varieties of salt do. Nevertheless, even natural salt must be eaten in moderation. To me it was very helpful to replace salt with fresh herbs in order to increase the flavor of my meals.

"Salt is like negative emotions. A little bit of salt improves the flavor. Too much salt makes it inedible. Watch how much salt you put in your life." – David Fishman

Sweeten your life… without risks

Added sugars, like sucrose (white table sugar, which comes from sugar cane or beets) and high fructose corn syrup, have many calories without providing essential nutrients because they have lost their nutritional properties in the processing that they have undergone. These sweeteners were tremendously harmful to my health. When products are refined, their proteins, fibers, essential fats, vitamins, and minerals tend to be removed, which is why they are labeled "empty" calories or "dead" products, as they don´t contain any necessary nutrients for the human body. These processed products also provide big profits for the industries that produce them because they last longer without going to waste, and, in many cases, become addictive.

The intake of too many sweeteners can cause cavities, obesity, type 2 diabetes, bad cholesterol, heart disease, fragility of the immune system, and many other health issues. According to the United States Department of Agriculture (USDA), "the average American consumes anywhere between150 and 170 pounds of simple sugars… per year. That is A LOT of sugar - especially when you compare to it how much we used to consume in the past. Less than 100 years ago, the average intake of sugar was only about 4 pounds per person per year."[40] On the other hand, the World Health Organization (WHO) "recommends adults and children

---

[40] "Profiling Food Consumption in America." United States Department of Agriculture, 2010.
http://www.usda.gov/factbook/chapter2.pdf

reduce their daily intake of free sugars to less than 10% of their total energy intake. A further reduction to below 5% or roughly 25 grams (6 teaspoons) per day would provide additional health benefits."[41] Even if the health benefits seem amazing, meeting this recommendation is practically impossible if you don't know the difference between natural sugar and processed sugar, as the latter is found in most of the food that we eat daily... and oftentimes we don't even realize that we're consuming processed sugars in our foods. We find it, for example, in foods made with white flour, in sodas and energy drinks, frozen foods, candy, breakfast cereals, cookies, jams, white and milk chocolates, dessert, dressings, and even tomato sauce.

I remember that my favorite breakfast used to be a donut accompanied by Fruit Loops cereal or waffles covered in syrup. A donut has nearly 11 grams of sugar, and a cup of Fruit Loops has around 12 grams (which makes up almost half of the amount of sugar that a person is advised to consume in a day). A waffle with ¼ cup of syrup contains around 35 grams of sugar. To

---

[41] "WHO Calls on Countries to Reduce Sugars Intake Among Adults and Children." World Health Organization, March. 4, 2015.
http://www.who.int/mediacentre/news/releases/2015/sugar-guideline/en/

this, I added a cup of coffee sweetened with two spoons of sugar. With such meals, I was basically starting my day already consuming much more than the daily recommendation suggested by the WHO. This kind of breakfast provided me with an "energy boost" that quickly plummeted, leaving me exhausted by midday. This caused me to need more sugar in order to keep working, and many times I ate a chocolate bar (which has approximately 14 grams of sugar) as the solution. My energy again rose, and when it dropped again I drank a couple of Coca Colas, or some other can of soda, which could have up to 40 grams of sugar per can! In contrast to refined/processed sugars, those sugars that come naturally from fruits and vegetables are gradually absorbed in the body and therefore don't cause spikes in blood sugar levels.

It is important to mention that liver function is severely affected by an excess of refined sugar, and this is a problem that seriously affects diabetics. According to the WHO, "globally, an estimated 422 million adults were living with diabetes in 2014," and "in 2012 there were 1.5 million deaths worldwide directly caused by diabetes. It was the eighth leading cause of death among both sexes and the fifth leading cause of death in women in 2012."[42] I have a very personal connection

---

[42] "Global Report on Diabetes," World Health Organization,

to this disease, as I have loved ones who suffer from it. The WHO explains that, "diabetes is a serious, chronic disease that occurs either when the pancreas does not produce enough insulin (a hormone that regulates blood sugar, or glucose), or when the body cannot effectively use the insulin it produces." [43] The effect of uncontrolled diabetes is the increase of sugar in the blood, known as hyperglycemia, which, over time, severely damages many organs and systems, especially the nerves and blood vessels. Diabetes can also cause damage to the heart, blood vessels, eyes, kidneys and nerves. In response to this global issue, "the World Health Assembly adopted a comprehensive global monitoring framework in 2013 comprised of nine voluntary global targets to reach by 2025... This was accompanied by the WHO Global action plan for the prevention and control of NCDs (non-communicable diseases) 2013 – 2020 (WHO NCD Global Action Plan), endorsed by the 66th World Health Assembly, which provides a roadmap and policy options to attain the nine voluntary global targets. Diabetes and its key risk factors are strongly reflected in the targets and indicators of the global monitoring framework and the

---

2016 6-7
http://apps.who.int/iris/bitstream/10665/204871/1/97892415652
57_eng.pdf
[43] "Global Report on Diabetes," 15

WHO NCD Global Action Plan."[44]

Many people who suffer from diabetes may not know that one of the liver´s jobs is to regulate blood sugar levels, in addition to storing and creating glucose, depending on what the body needs. At research done at Duke University, it was found that, "obese people who consume increased amounts of fructose, a type of sugar that is found in particular in soft drinks and commercial fruit juices, are at risk for nonalcoholic fatty liver disease (NFALD) and its more severe forms, fatty inflammation and scarring." [45] Among the main symptoms of this disease are: pain in the upper right abdomen, chronic fatigue, general discomfort and fullness after meals.

In general, the constant intake of refined sugars can cause damage to all body systems. So, in accordance with the saying, "better to prevent than to cure," I am going to provide you with a detailed description of the different kinds of refined sugars so that you can identify

---

[44] "Global Report on Diabetes," 6-16

[45] "Increased Fructose Consumption May Deplete Cellular Energy in Patients with Obesity and Diabetes," Duke Health, May 2, 20112. dukehealth.org
https://corporate.dukehealth.org/news-listing/increased-fructose-consumption-may-deplete-cellular-energy-patients-obesity-and-diabetes

them and avoid them, or, at the very least, reduce them: White sugar: This is the table sugar that comes from sugar cane or beets. It is 100% refined and lacks nutrients, vitamins, and minerals. It contains 99% sucralose.

Brown sugar: This is also refined and contains 95% sucralose. It´s brown in color due to the presence of molasses. It contains 5% mineral salts and organic substances, which give it a moist appearance and its scent. It has very few vitamins and is used, among other things, to caramelize.

Raw sugar: A very aromatic kind of sugar that, according to its brewing level, can be blond or brown. It´s generally used to sweeten crepes and waffles, among other baked goods.

Rapadura: This is an unrefined cane sugar and is usually sold only in health food shops. It has a granular texture rather than a crystallized one because it not as heavily processed as white sugar. It adds a lot of sweetness to foods that it is used with.

Molasses: This is a kind of syrup like the one we use on pancakes, but it is more viscous, as it is concentrated from refined sugar cane. It has fewer calories than white sugar and a higher content of minerals and vitamins. It is generally used in baking and to add color to foods.

Artificial or synthetic sweeteners: These are created artificially by men, rather than occurring naturally. They have a lower amount of calories but are often as harmful or even more so than refined sugar. They are used to sweeten all diet beverages, including sodas, and low calorie foods, sweets, and candies. A widely used sweetener is high fructose corn syrup, which is obtained by processing corn. We find it in almost every sweet product, and it frequently comes from GMO corn, especially in the United States. (I don't want to get ahead of myself, but later on we will talk more about GMO products, or products that have been genetically altered). This syrup is related to the obesity epidemic in the United States and is very bad for one's health. Among artificial sweeteners, there are also aspartame (which is in Equal and NutraSweet), sucralose (or Splenda), Saccharin (which is in Sweet N' Low and Nectasweet), and Acesulfame (which is in Sunett and Sweet One). Even though these products are advertised as an alternative to sugar and are even recommended for those who want to lose weight or who suffer from diabetes, they are equally or even more harmful for our health than sugar.

There is much research that proves the hazardous

effects that aspartame, in particular, causes to the body. One study warns that, once aspartame enters the body, it breaks up into three very dangerous poisons: methanol, aspartic acid (which decreases the absorption of magnesium and therefore compromises the absorption of vitamin D), and phenylalanine (an amino acid responsible for the sweet flavor of aspartame) that lower the immune system's defenses and could even cause brain damage and cancer. [46] Aspartame is no longer used by several companies that have recognized its toxic potential, including Pepsi. A *Washington Post* article, published on April 27th of 2015, stated that, "PepsiCo Inc., the maker of Pepsi, Mountain Dew, and many other popular soft drinks, is changing the formula of one of its offerings for the first time in decades.. The company said Friday it will stop sweetening Diet Pepsi, Caffeine Free Diet Pepsi, and Wild Cherry Diet Pepsi with aspartame, a controversial artificial sweetener. Beginning in August, the drinks will instead come sweetened with Sucralose, better known as Splenda, and acesulfame potassium, which is often called Ace K and

---

[46] Morando, Soffritti., Belpoggi, Fiorella., Tibaldi, Eva., et al., "Life-Span Exposure to Low Doses of Aspartame Beginning During Prenatal Life Increases Cancer Effects in Rats," Environmental Health Perspective, 115 (2007): 1293-1297

is currently used in Coke Zero."[47]

Famous doctor Joseph Mercola, who is trained in traditional and natural medicine, has written several books and articles wherein he mentions a compilation of studies that relate the use of artificial sweeteners with cancer, allergies, weight gain, vision and hearing problems, brain and nervous system damage, memory problems, convulsions, and negative effects at cellular level.[48] Overall, our bodies do not recognize these kinds of synthetic sweeteners as compatible, and so they make us sick.

"The food you eat can be either the safest and most powerful form of medicine, or the slowest form of poison." – Ann Wigmore.

Unlike processed sugar and additives, natural sugar is necessary for your body, as it provides energy and enables good muscle and brain function. It also absorbs

---

[47] Ferdman, Robert., "Why Pepsi's decision to Ditch Aspartame Isn't Good for Soda or Science," washingtonpost.com, April, 27, 2015. https://www.washingtonpost.com/news/wonk/wp/2015/04/27/why-pepsis-decision-to-ditch-aspartame-isnt-good-for-soda-or-science/

[48] Dr. Mercola., "Splenda: It Can Destroy Your Immune System and Is Like Eating an Insecticide" Nov. 10, 2011. mercola.com https://goo.gl/yrnZhH

more easily because the foods that natural sugars are in contain vitamins, minerals, and fiber that aid in their breakdown. In other words, your body takes what it needs and eliminates any excess. This type of sugar is found in whole, unprocessed foods, like fruits (apples, watermelon, figs, strawberries, pineapple, papaya, oranges, pears, bananas, and mangos), whole grains and cereals (wheat, rye, rice, oatmeal, and barley), milk (lactose), and vegetables (beets, carrots, onions, turnips, eggplant, and tomatoes). Other natural sugars include:

Honey: A fluid produced by bees from the nectar of flowers. It´s a popular food and very well known for its medicinal properties because it cleanses the blood, relieves throat irritation and inflammation, rejuvenates the skin, and helps with seasonal allergies if it is a local variety.

Maple Syrup: This sweetener has a particular and scented flavor, and it comes from the concentration of maple sap. The best quality maple syrup is C grade (originally from Canada) because it has preserved all of its nutritional characteristics. Be weary of fake maple syrups because they are made of sugared glucose and are artificially colored.

Agave syrup: This sweetener is also known as agave nectar, as it is extracted from the leaves of the agave plant. Many nutritionists and homeopaths prescribe it as an alternative to sugar. It is low in calories and has a potent sweetening power.

Stevia syrup: This sweetener is also obtained from a plant—one that grows in South America. It has 0 calories and is a powerful sweetener, though its effects on the body are still up for debate.

The more aware I became of the effect of sugars on the body, the more incredulous I was at how all of the foods that I ate were contributing to my disease. Little by little, I started to make small changes. For example, I replaced my morning donut with whole grain toast and the cookies and sweets with fruit. Even if it was a little hard at first because I was completely addicted to sugar, I started noticing that by adding natural sugar into my diet, my craving for sweets gradually began to disappear. This was because my body was receiving the vitamins that it needed, so it didn't crave refined sugars to "feel good." Unfortunately, there are many diets designed to lose weight that restrict the use of natural sugar, which increases the possibilities for anxiety and depression. This is also when people turn to artificial sweeteners and refined sweets. Another thing that I did was to reduce my coffee intake and add more green tea to my diet, which has many benefits for our health, among them the reduction of inflammation and stress.

Along with the above efforts, I substituted juices and cola drinks with water. To be honest, I knew that water consumption was a necessity, but I had never thought about how important it is in maintaining good health. Our body is made up of 70% of water, and drinking water is a great way to reduce inflammation in the body because it helps it to flush out toxins and other irritants. Indeed, water helps all bodily functions to occur. I try to drink at least eight to nine glasses of water daily because being dehydrated can be very harmful for our health. To illustrate, a report published by the *Clinical Nutrition and Hospital Diet* magazine informs us that:

- Two percent or more rate of dehydration induced by exercise or high temperature implies a decrease of short-term memory, aim, motor visual tracking, attention, arithmetic efficiency, and reaction time.

- Moderate degrees of dehydration, situated at an interval of 2.5 to 2.8% of loss of body weight, imply significant changes in cognitive ability and attention span, and in the progressive increase of physical and mental fatigue.

- Three percent rate of dehydration leads to a decrease of cerebral blood flow and is enough to induce cognitive disorientation and headaches.

- At a four percent rate of dehydration, motor speeds show a greater decrease, while at six percent dehydration, it is frequent to experience delirium and/or hallucinations. [49]

I want to make clear that these changes didn't happen all of a sudden. It took me time and patience. My motivation to heal myself helped me to keep learning and modifying my diet. Recognizing that my body got better little by little was the sign that I was on the right path, and that gave me the strength to keep going.

"Part of healing is in the will to heal." – Lucio Anneo Séneca

Trans Fats? No, thank you

After I had eliminated sugars, fats followed. Unfortunately, the fats with which processed meals and fast foods are made are also very harmful to our health.

---

[49] Martinez, Alvarez., Marin, Villarino., Allue, Polanco., et al., "Recomendaciones de Bebida e Hidratación Para La Población Española," Nutrición Clínica Y Dietética Hospitalaria, (2008): 3-19. http://www.nutricion.org/publicaciones/revistas/Nutr ClinDietHosp08(28)2_3_19.pdf

One such example is hydrogenated oils, or trans fats, that are not natural and come from human manipulation, wherein a chemical procedure solidifies oils through the addition of hydrogen at high pressures and temperatures. With this method, oils like palm oil are heated and then quickly cooled down again, separating their liquid parts from their solid ones, and keeping only the part that contains the worse fats for the body (those that are concentrated). In the same way, another oils like corn or canola, which are essentially very healthy, are heated up to more than a thousand degrees and turned into preservatives. Companies sell them as 100% vegetable oil, which causes the consumer to think that they are healthy oils, but in actuality, even if they come from a vegetable, when they go through the hydrogenation process, they became transformed fats. Manufacturers use them because of their low cost and long shelf life, for these fats can be kept much longer without expiring. This way, meals can be kept "fresh" for a greater period.

According to the World Health Organization, "consumption of trans fats is associated with an increased risk of noncommunicable diseases, including cardiovascular disease, such as heart disease, as well as stroke and diabetes. These partially hydrogenated vegetable oils are, however, favoured by the food industry and fast food outlets because they are cheap, have a long shelf life, are semisolid at room temperature, which makes them easier to use in baked products, and can withstand repeated heating." [50]

The banning of trans fats from foods was included in the Action Plan for Prevention and Control of Non-Communicable Diseases of the WHO, which was addressed by the global council in 2013. Even so, though some companies deny their use, labeling products with "zero trans," the FDA states that foods may contain up to a half gram of trans fats and still be labeled as "zero trans." So, when you see a product that mentions that it has partially hydrogenated oil or vegetable oil, try to replace it with a healthier choice, especially if it is something that you consume regularly. I must mention here that even if "by law" it is mandatory to inform the consumer about trans-fat contents in the food, this is not required in restaurants, since these don't always have to provide nutritional information about the meals that they serve. Usually, restaurants use these kinds of fats for frying and baking. This is why when my family and I eat out, and we don't know if the restaurant is truly reliable, we try to order dishes that have been steamed, followed by fresh fruits

---

[50] Evidence Piles Up for Banning Trans Fat," <u>World Health Organization</u>, April, 2013.
http://www.who.int/bulletin/releases/NFM0413/en/

as dessert.

Color it up!

Other elements that are added to processed meals and fast food are artificial colors and preservatives. Colors lack nutritional qualities and are only used to add color and improve the esthetic look of the product. As a result, the food looks fresher and therefore "healthy" and more appealing, especially the products that we give children. The list of color additives is huge, but the ones that are most frequently used in the United States are Blue 1, Blue 2, Red 40, Yellow 5, and Yellow 6. I had always thought that color additives came from fruits, vegetables, or herbs, like saffron or beets, when in fact these artificial colors are derivatives from charcoal and petroleum. Some of the main consequences of artificial colorings are allergies, asthma, and a decrease in the immune system's abilities to battle diseases.

I had no idea that many of the foods that I ingested daily were filled with artificial colors. For example, Blue 1 and Blue 2 are mainly used in precooked food and desserts, and consumption of these additives can lead to cancer and masculine infertility. Red 40 is one of the most consumed colors, and it is used in cereals, sauces, snacks, chips, sodas, precooked foods, sweets like

M&M's, jellies, condiments, cosmetic products, and even certain medicines. It is added to many meals in order to make them look fresh and appealing. The compounds of the red coloring, benzidine and amino biphenyl, have been related to cancer, liver problems, stomach ailments, colon diseases, irritability, and hyperactivity, especially in children. Yellow 5 is found in custards, sodas, ice creams, sweets, cereals, instant noodles, and jams and could cause allergic reactions, asthma attacks, migraines, vision problems, and anxiety. Yellow 6 is in cereals, snacks, ice creams, sodas, candy, sausages, jellies, and bakery products. It can lead to renal and suprarenal gland tumors. Hence, several countries in Europe and the United Kingdom have forbidden the use of such color additives. [51]

A study published by the Center for Science in the Public Interest (CSPI) "reports on the dye content of scores of breakfast cereals, candies, baked goods, and other foods… The findings are disturbing since the amounts of dyes found in even single servings of numerous foods—or combinations of several dyed foods—are higher than the levels demonstrated in some clinical trials to impair some children's behavior."

---

[51] Kim, Susana. "11 Foods Ingredients Banned Outside the U.S. That We Eat," June, 26, 2013. abcnews.go.com.http://abcnews.go.com/Lifestyle/Food/11-foods-banned-us/story?id=19457237

[52] In another article, also published by CSPI, they highlight that, "food dyes, synthesized originally from coal tar and now petroleum, have long been controversial. Many dyes have been banned because of their adverse effects on laboratory animals…[but] many of the nine currently approved dyes raise health concerns." [53] The same article tells us that "in addition to considerations of organ damage, cancer, birth defects, and allergic reactions, mixtures of dyes (and Yellow 5 tested alone) cause hyperactivity and other behavioral problems in some children," plus experiments in laboratory animals with Blue 1, Blue 2, Green 3, Red 40, Yellow 5 and Yellow 6 showed signs of causing cancer and various ailments, and Yellow also caused mutations in six of the 11 studies. [54] James Huff, associated director for the study of chemical carcinogenesis in the National Institute of Environmental Health Sciences' National Toxicology Program, points out that, "dyes add no benefits whatsoever to foods, other than making them more

---

[52] "First-Ever Study Reveals Amounts of Foods Dyes In Brand-Names Foods," Center for Science in the Public Interest, May 7, 2014, https://cspinet.org/new/201405071.html
[53] "Food Dyes: A Rainbow of Risk," Center for Science in the Public Interest, June 1, 2010. V-1
https://cspinet.org/new/pdf/food-dyes-rainbow-of-risks.pdf
[54] "Food Dyes: A Rainbow of Risks," 13-16

'eye-catching' to increase sales." [55]

In 2001, the government agency that controls the quality of American food and medicines, the Food and Drug Administration (FDA), accepted that color additives are harmful for health and so forced companies that produce them to alert the consumers of their presence on food labels. Despite the fact that the FDA admits that color additives are harmful for health, their sale was not forbidden, and many companies continue to use them. Therefore, it is very important that we know how to read labels and distinguish these color additives in order to try to avoid their intake. I know that it is hard to memorize the different kinds of harmful additives, and knowing how to differentiate the natural ones from the ones that aren't takes some work, but I recommend that when reading food labels, try to make sure that if they have some kind of color added, it comes from a natural source, like those that come mainly from fruits and vegetables, and not those that say that they contain artificial colors.

---

[55] "CSPI Says Food Dyes Pose Rainbow of Risks: Cancer, Hyperactivity, Allergic Reactions," Center for Science In The Public Interest, June 29, 2010. 1-2
https://cspinet.org/new/201006291.html

P is for preservatives and poor health

Preservatives, used to help food last for a long period of time, can also cause chronic illnesses of the mind and body. The more I read, the more horror I felt about the dangers of preservatives in food. For example, a study conducted by the Cancer Research Center in Hawaii and South California University informs us that, "red and processed meat intakes were associated with an increased risk of pancreatic cancer... Carcinogenic substances related to meat preparation methods might be responsible for the positive association;" in other words, sodium nitrates and nitrites (commonly used in processed meats like bacon, ham, hot dogs, salami, sausages, smoked fish, and canned meats) may cause cancer of the pancreas or colon. [56] Another study showed that "maternal consumption of nitrite-cured meats during pregnancy increased the risk of brain tumors in children." [57]

---

[56] Nöthlings, Ute, Wilkens, Lynne R., Murphy, Suzanne., et al., "Meat and Fat Intake as Risk Factors for Pancreatic Cancer: The Multiethnic Cohort Study," Journal of the National Cancer Institute 97 (2005): 1458-1465. http://jnci.oxfordjournals.org/content/97/19/1458.full

[57] Savitz, David. Sarasua, Sara. "Cured and Broiled Meat Consumption in Relation to Childhood Cancer," Journal of Cancer Causes and Control, 5 (1994): 141-148

Another reason why I reduced my consumption of fast food is that they mostly offer food that is full of additives, artificial colors, and preservatives. Here is a list of the most commonly used preservatives and their possible side effects. It is almost impossible to entirely avoid these ingredients, because they are practically everywhere, but once you can identify them, it is easier to control their intake:

- Sodium benzoate is used to stop the growth of bacteria and fungi in vinegars, carbonated drinks, jams, fruit juices, soy sauce, mustard, and sodas like Coke and Sprite, among others. When it is mixed with vitamin C or ascorbic acid, a compound called benzene is formed; this is a known carcinogen.

- Sodium Nitrate (E-251), Sodium Nitrite (E-250), Potassium Nitrate (E-252), and Potassium Nitrite (E-249) are used in meats to maintain their color and flavor. They destroy red blood cells and are carcinogenic.

- Sulphites (From E- 226 to E-227) are used in some wines and fruits to prevent the growth of bacteria and fermentation. They cause allergic reactions in many people, and this reaction can, though rarely, be fatal.

- BHA and BHT (E-320 and E- 321) preserve fats so that they don't become rancid. These can cause hyperactivity, angioedema, asthma, rhinitis, dermatitis, hives, and tumors. Something very interesting about this additive is that the state of California recognized it as a possible carcinogen, but didn't forbid it, while England and other European countries have banned it.

- Propyl gallate also inhibits fats and oils from going bad. Sometimes it is found in products like chicken soup, chewing gum, and meat. It too causes cancer.

GMO: OMG! (Oh, my God!)

Other products that are harmful for our health and that have been controversial in recent years are foods sprayed with herbicides and pesticides and the seeds of GMO (Genetically Modified Organism) food. Herbicides and pesticides are used to control the invasion of parasites, insects, and other pests that might harm crops. These chemical poisons imitate estrogen hormones and when consumed in certain quantities can increase the frequency of breast cancer and uterine tumors, among other complications. They are particularly dangerous during pregnancy and childhood. They are also linked to kidney and liver damage, problems in reproduction, and disruption of hormonal balance. In studies conducted at the Parkinson-ICP Institute in Milan, Italy, by Gianni Pezzoli and Emanuele Cereda, clear links were found between the use of herbicides and pesticides in agriculture and the development of Parkinson´s disease. One of the results of the investigation was that "exposure to pesticides or solvents [increases the] risk factor for [Parkinson's disease]" by between 33 and an 80 percent. [58]

The Internal Agency for Research on Cancer, which is the specialized cancer agency of the World Health Organization, points out the carcinogenic possibilities of five pesticides: "The herbicide glyphosate [which causes cancer in laboratory animals] and the insecticides malathion [also causes cancer in laboratory animals] and diazinon were classified as probably carcinogenic to humans... The insecticides tetrachlorvinphos [which are forbidden in Europe, but not the U.S.] and parathion [which also causes cancer in laboratory

---

[58] Cereda, Emanuelle., Pezzoli, Gianni., "Exposure to Pesticides or Solvents and Risks of Parkinson Disease," Journal of the American Academy of Neurology, 80 (2013) 2035-2041

animals] were classified as possibly carcinogenic to humans... For the insecticide malathion, there is limited evidence of carcinogenicity in humans for non Hodgkin lymphoma and prostate cancer... For the insecticide diazinon, there was limited evidence of carcinogenicity in humans for non-Hodgkin lymphoma and lung cancer." [59]

The following is a list of the most common herbicides and pesticides:

- Organochlorine pesticides: DDT, DDE, Chlordane, Heptachlor, Dieldrin, Methoxane

- Organophosphate pesticides: Diazinon, chlorpyrifos

- Atrazine herbicides: Atrazine, simazine, cyanazine

- Chlorophenoxyl herbicides: 2, 4-D, 2,4, 5-T, Agent Orange.

---

[59] Evaluation of Five Organophosphate Insecticides and Herbicides," International Agency for Research on Cancer Monographs 112, March 20, 2015. 1-2 https://www.iarc.fr/en/media-centre/iarcnews/pdf/Monograph Volume112.pdf

Another reason that I reduced processed foods was learning about GMO products and the damage that they can do to our bodies. GMOs are organisms whose DNA have been altered by scientists using genetic engineering techniques, like adding some other food´s DNA to introduce a new feature into a food source. During this process, gene manipulation occurs, like when bacteria and viruses (from vegetables, humans, or animals) are introduced into the DNA of food or animals. So, people (rather than nature) mixes genes of certain species with the genes of other species, so that something entirely new emerges, with characteristics that were nonexistent in that food source until the manipulation occurred. This technique allows scientists to create certain plants that demonstrate better resistance to the viruses and plagues that attack them and to extreme temperatures that might stunt or end their growth; this allows agribusiness to be able to grow vegetables and fruits in places where they would never survive otherwise. Their size and reproduction capabilities can also be increased to very large quantities using genetic modification. Given that this food does not grow naturally, our body doesn't recognize it, making it very hard to digest, process, and use. This creates very serious health problems because the body doesn't have the means to process what it has ingested, which can lead to diseases like cancer, immune diseases, infections, non-controllable viruses, sterility, and birth defects.

The most common GMO foods in the United States are:

- High fructose corn syrup, which is a main ingredient in sodas, bakery items, and frozen foods.

- Corn, 95% of which is GMO. In addition to being included in many cereals, it is the basic food staple of many animals that are raised for consumption, including the sources of dairy products, meat, eggs, etc.

- Vegetable oils come from different plants, and the most popular types are canola, cotton seed, and rapeseed (where canola oil comes from).

- Soy and its derivatives (milk, flour, tofu, sauce, etc.). In its natural state, soy is a very nutritional food with anti-carcinogenic properties. It has been one of basic foodstuffs in Asia for years. Unfortunately, the vast majority of soy is now GMO, and it thus loses all of its beneficial properties and becomes more harmful for our bodies.

- Papaya (from Hawaii).

- Beet sugar.

Unfortunately, many people in the United States aren't aware of most of the GMO products that are currently on the market because the companies that produce them spend millions of dollars making sure that the consumer remains unaware that the foods are GMOs. This problem doesn't only exist in this country, as these seeds are exported to many countries around the world. The use of GMOs has been intensely debated for some time. There are many activists who are seriously concerned about the diseases that these products might bring to the environment and to human beings, and so they have started demanding that their use is specified on food labels. In 2012 in California, Preposition 37, which forced the labeling of GMOs, wasn't approved, and a similar measure was defeated in Washington in 2015. In both campaigns, the companies primarily responsible for the use of GMOs, Monsanto, DuPont, and Dow Chemical, used extensive publicity and money to help defeat these proposals. These biotechnology companies argue that the GMO seeds increase crop performance and save farmers time and money by reducing the use of pesticides and herbicides while also helping to reduce global hunger. However, in many countries, the use of GMOs has been forbidden, as is the case in " Switzerland, Australia, Austria, China, India, France, Germany, Hungary, Luxembourg, Greece, Bulgaria, Poland, Italy, Mexico and Russia" [60] Recently, Mexico forbade the GMO seed for corn as well.

I remember the first time that I became aware of the damages caused by GMO products; I read an article published in 2012 by the Journal of Food and Chemical Toxicology, which mentioned a study done by the French scientist Gilles-Eric Seralini. In this study, the researchers noted the atrocious effects that Roundup-tolerant genetically modified corn had on rats, including severe alteration in liver and kidney health, changes in hormonal systems, the development of tumors, and early death. [61] This study received considerable criticism from the supporters of GMO products, to the extent that a year later, the magazine (*FCT*) withdrew the investigation, claiming that it was "faulty." However, many scientists supported the result of this investigation and blamed Monsanto for applying strong

---

[60] Bello, Walden., 'Twenty-Six Countries Ban GMOs-Why Won't the U.S.?" The Nation October 29, 2013. https://www.the nation.com/article/twenty-six-countries-ban-gmos-why-wont-us/
[61] Seralini, Gilles-eric., Clair, Emilie., Mesnage, R., et al., "Retracted: Long Term Toxicity of a Roundup Herbicide and a Roundup-Tolerant Genetically Modified Maize," Food and Chemical Toxicology, 50 (2012) 4221-4231

corporate pressure and paying their researchers to discredit the experiment. [62] After several revisions by scientific boards, this investigation was declared valid and was republished in 2014 in the Environmental Sciences Europe publication. While I was informing myself about this very important part of my diet, I found another study conducted in Brazil in 2009, where for 15 months a group of rats was fed with GMO soy. At the end of the experiment, the study found that rats presented significant changes in their reproductive systems and uteri compared to the rats that hadn't consumed soy and the ones that had been fed with organic soy. [63]

---

[62] Gilles-Eric Séralini., Robin Mesnage., Nicolas Defarge., Joël Spiroux de Vendômois., "Conflicts of Interests, Confidentiality and Censorship in Health Risk Assessment: The Example of An Herbicide and A GMO," Environmental Sciences Europe, 26 (1), (2014):1

[63] Flávia, Brasil., Lavínia, Soares., Tatiane, Faria., et al., "The Impact of Dietary Organic and Transgenic Soy on the Reproductive System of Female Adult Rat," The Anatomical Record Journal, 292 (2009), 587-594

Some of these changes were:

- Excessive production of estrogen, progesterone, and follicle-stimulating and luteinizing hormones in the reproductive hormones.

- Damages in the pituitary gland.

- Backward menstrual flow, meaning that it travels in the opposite direction from the natural one towards the uterus, which can cause endometriosis, infertility, pelvic pains, gastrointestinal problems, and chronic fatigue, among other ailments.

- Damaged sperms cells and other changes in the testicles.

I repeat again that my point isn't to criticize these companies, but it is important to know that GMOs aren't made by Mother Nature, but rather by the hand of engineers. When eating these foods, your body receives them as strange objects, and your immune system starts attacking them, creating an inflammatory reaction. As I mentioned earlier, chronic inflammation leads to countless diseases. I recommend that you do research about this topic and draw your own conclusions.

A great advantage of consuming organic products is that you don't have to worry about any kind of color additives, preservatives, herbicides, pesticides, or GMO seeds because their use in these foods is forbidden. I want to share two pieces of advice from author and professor Michael Pollan, from University of California Berkeley, who remains at the forefront of the healthy food movement in the United States:

- Don't eat food that doesn't rot. Junk food and fast food don't rot easily because they are filled with additives and other chemical substances that preserve them. If it doesn't rot, it isn't food.

- Eat only food what your grandmother would buy. If the label can't be read because it has a lot of chemical names, it's better to avoid it.

"Let food be thy medicine and medicine be thy food." – Hippocrates.

While I was detoxing my body from all of the aforementioned products, I nourished it with real food, made by nature and filled with vitamins and minerals, like fruits, vegetables, whole grains, protein, and healthy fats. There are many people who consume an unnecessary amount of vitamins and minerals in the shape of pills and then think that this is enough for their bodies, but it isn't. While it is true that, in some cases, we can benefit from vitamin, mineral, or protein supplements, all that our body needs can be found in our food. And none of the vitamin and mineral pills offer what real food offers: carotenoids and flavonoids. What are these? Carotenoids are organic pigments that have antioxidants and anti-carcinogenic properties. They are naturally found in plants, algae, some kinds of fungi, and certain bacteria. They are responsible for most of the yellow, orange, and red colors present in vegetable-based foods, and for the orange colors in several animal foods. Among them we find vitamin A and B carotene (in carrots, for example), lycopene (in tomatoes), astaxanthin (in prawns), b-cryptoxanthin (in oranges), capsanthin (in fresh pepper, dry pepper, paprika), and lutein (in green beans, spinach, broccoli). In addition to their anti carcinogenic properties, carotenoids aid the prevention of heart disease, increase the defenses of the immune system, protect cell membranes, are good for the memory, and prevent cataracts and macular degeneration.

Flavonoids are natural compounds that are present in vegetables, fruit, seeds, flowers, red wine, green tea, black tea, cacao, and soy. flavonoids are an excellent source of antioxidants that protect the circulatory system. According to the American Journal of Clinical

Nutrition, drinking three cups of black tea per day could aid the prevention of cardiovascular diseases. [64] Flavonoids in general have a great number of antioxidants and help prevent dementia and Alzheimer's, slow aging, reduce inflammation, prevent cavities, combat viruses, improve arterial health, and have anti-carcinogenic properties. In addition to the sources mentioned above, apples, cranberries, broccoli, pears, kiwi, cabbage, onions, strawberries, and red grapes are good sources of flavonoids. When I realized this, I started adding more fruits and vegetables into my life…

Fruits and Vegetables: The winning team

Fruits and vegetables are "real" food because they contain water, vitamins, minerals, fibers, and nutrients that help us to maintain a healthy body. Having a diet that is rich and varied in fruit and vegetables contributes to the decrease of cardiac diseases, inflammation, cancer, diabetes, digestive and stomach

---

[64] Grassi, Davide., Desideri, Giovambattista., Di Giosia, Paolo., De Feo, Martina., et al., "Tea, Flavonoids, and Cardiovascular Health: Endothelial Protection," The American Journal of Clinical Nutrition, (2013): 1-7 http://ajcn.nutrition.org/content/early/2013/10/30/ajcn.113.058313.full.pdf

problems, and strokes. It also contributes to the maintenance of a healthy weight because these foods are low in calories and fats and help the body to feel full longer. The U.S. Department of Agriculture recommends eating three to five servings of fruits daily, but the average is three servings per day. I always try to keep fruits and vegetables in a visible spot, and I like to have a variety of them at home. When I go to the market, I explore new possibilities, then try to cook food that has vegetables. I also try to eat at least a salad each day, to which I also add fruits sometimes.

In an article published on the OMS web-page, they inform us that, "in general, it is calculated that 1.7 million lives could be saved each year if the intake of fruits and vegetables was increased enough. The Global OMS Strategy on Alimentary Regime, Physical Activity and Health highlights the increase of fruit and vegetable intake as one of the recommendations to consider when developing national dietary policies and guidelines for both the community and individuals." [65] Most fruits and vegetables haven't been processed and are ready to eat. I recommend buying organic ones, or at least the

---

[65] "Estrategia Mundial Sobre Régimen Alimentario, Actividad Física Y Salud," Organización Mundial de la Salud, (2004), 1-24.http://www.who.int/dietphysicalactivity/strategy/eb11344/strategy_spanish_web.pdf

ones that are local products and free of pesticides and chemicals. Try reducing those that come in cans or are frozen because they have been processed and are no longer pure, even if they are organic.

To me, it is important to create a rainbow of fruits and vegetables in my diet, but green vegetables usually have more nutritional value than the others. In any case, don't discard the others because each one plays a specific role in maintaining our health. For example, carrots, which are rich in vitamin A, are very good for sight, and beets can help to maintain a healthy liver (these two combined in a salad or juice are very tasty). Green fruits and vegetables are very good to detox the body, and yellow ones contain vitamin C and keep the immune system strong.

Whole Grains: Key for Digestion

Fiber is very good for digestion and essential for health. Many times, when we go to the doctor with pain in our digestive systems, they recommend eating more fiber. Whole grains not only give us the fiber that the body needs, but also give us vitamins, minerals, and antioxidants. Fiber is also prescribed to fight constipation due to its ability to absorb water and prevent obesity, as high-fiber foods contain fewer calories and produce the feeling of fullness. A low-fiber diet predisposes the body to the development of cancer, diabetes, heart problems, obesity, inflammation, and arthritis.

In an article published by Sanitas, the Spanish group of health assistance and wellbeing, they found that, "another positive effect of this kind of fiber (soluble) is that it reduces fat and sugar absorption in the body, so it plays a role in cardiovascular protection by controlling cholesterol, triglycerides, and glucose… fiber plays a very important role in diets designed to reduce weight, especially due to its satiating effect and its capacity to avoid constipation. Besides, diets rich in fiber have a lower caloric value." [66] Among the whole grains that are good for you are: corn, wheat, amaranth, barley, bulgur, millet, quinoa, rye, brown rice, kamut, oatmeal, spelt, and sorghum. Try consuming organic corn because GMOs are commonplace. Among the grains, only corn currently contains known GMOs, but it is difficult to know if other grains contain GMOs, as I explained before, because companies that produce them don't provide any specifications on their content.

Whole grains are made of germ, bran, and endosperm.

---

[66] "La fibra en la prevención de la obesidad," Sanita Más Salud, http://www.sanitas.es/sanitas/seguros/es/particulares/seguros_me dicos/cuadro_medico/sanitas-mas-salud/resumen/index.html

Germ and bran are the most nutritional parts of the grain because they contain all of the fiber, vitamins, minerals, and antioxidants. Unfortunately, during the refining process, the germ and bran are removed from the grain, leaving only the sugar (endosperm). This is how white flours are created out of wheat. White flours are commonly used in most of the food that we eat daily, like bread, pastas, and processed foods. Similarly, white rice comes from the processing of brown rice. Regularly eating these processed foods can cause obesity and predisposes the body to a myriad of diseases.

In the United States, many people's diet consists of refined products like hamburgers made with white bread, pasta, and processed or fast food. It is important to mention that Americans get sick more frequently than Europeans and people from other industrialized countries. In fact, the United States is one of the last countries to appear in the inferior part of a graph of global statistics regarding cardiopulmonary diseases, diabetes, obesity and disability. Its location on the graph is informed by the fact that the citizens are considered high risk in the development of such illnesses. This was very interesting to me because in the United States a lot of money is spent on health care, and yet it is one of the countries where people get sick more frequently.

With regard to processed foods, I never imagined that you could take all of the nutrients out of the food that is naturally so good for your body. Here again we see the hand of big companies at work because processed products are kept for a long time without damage and can be exported to remote parts of the planet. Companies market them as "healthy," and there is no law that penalizes them for such claims. For example, in the case of bread, there are many types that are sold as "enriched." This doesn't mean that they left the nutrients in the product, but rather that some vitamins have been added to make the public believe that they are better than regular bread; they can also charge more for them this way. This also happens with the ones that say "multigrain." If the product that you buy doesn't list "whole grain" as its first ingredient, then the grain has been refined.

The truth is that I have always loved white rice, and when I started replacing it with the brown variety, the flavor seemed strange to me, and it was harder to chew, but the more I ate it, the more my craving for processed products lessened. Now, if I eat too much white rice or too many cookies, I start feeling bloated and lethargic, whereas if I eat whole foods, my stomach feels good, my digestive health is excellent, and I enjoy an optimal level of energy. Obviously, each body is different. Let's take, for example, those who suffer celiac disease, which is a disease of the immune system that causes people to be unable to consume gluten (a protein present mainly in wheat, oatmeal, barley, and rye) because it damages their small intestine. Celiacs are allergic to those cereals but can choose other options, like quinoa, that are very good and easy to prepare. It is very important to consume grains, even though are many types of modern diets that recommend not eating carbohydrates, a component of the grains. The truth is that the fiber in grains is essential to losing and maintaining weight and promoting healthy digestion.

When you decide to start substituting refined/processed products for those that are more beneficial and natural, do it gradually so that it becomes easier for you and you avoid frustration. You can start adding healthy food to your meals, even if you´re still eating processed ones. After a short time, you´ll start to see how the processed food no longer seems so appealing, and you´ll start leaving it aside. As the saying goes, "you only have one body; feed it properly and it will return the favor."

Myths and truths about proteins

Proteins are macromolecules that act as the most important nutrient for the formation of muscles, ligaments, tendons, organs, nails, hair, and bodily fluids.

Among other things, they serve a defensive function because they create antibodies, in addition to providing energy and contributing to bone formation. In the past, an essential component of my diet was meat, whether it was from cows, chickens, or pigs. It was my main dish at both lunch and dinner. I felt that if I hadn't eaten meat, my meal was incomplete. Generally, almost all of my diet was based on animal derivatives: bread with cheese at breakfast, hamburgers for lunch, meat with white rice for dinner. I normally didn't eat fish and vegetables. I remember many of the articles that I read explained how a high-protein diet, especially those centered on animals products, could lead to osteoporosis, inflammation, kidney disease, urinary problems, and cancer, mainly in the intestines. Due to this and other reasons that I will explain later, little by little I started reducing my consumption of protein that came from animals and instead added protein that are sourced from plants and fish.

Many people think that eating animal proteins is essential in every meal, especially in the United States where the intake of proteins that come from animals is generally double the recommended serving. The World Health Organization states that at least 30% of the cases of cancer in Western countries and 20% of those in the developing countries have their roots in the citizens' diets. The Physicians Committee for

Responsible Medicine, which is a non-profit based in Washington D.C. that works to adhere to the highest standards of ethics and efficiency in research, published an article that stated that there are two common topics in the results of studies that have been made about cancer in various parts of the world: first, that fruits and vegetables help reduce the risk of cancer, and second, that meat, animal products, and other fatty foods tend to increase the risk of cancer. The same article explains that this is because, "[fat] increases hormone production and thus raises breast cancer risks. It also stimulates the production of bile acids which have been linked to colon cancer" while "all the evidence points to a low-fat, high-fiber diet that includes a variety of fruits, vegetables, whole grains, and beans, as being the best for cancer prevention. Not surprisingly, vegetarians, whose diets easily meet these requirements, are at the lowest risk for cancer. Vegetarians have about half the cancer risk of meat-eaters." [67] About fiber, the article says, "fiber cannot be digested by humans early in the digestive process. It moves food more quickly through the intestines, helping to eliminate carcinogens. It also draws water into the digestive tract. The water and fiber make fecal matter bulkier, so carcinogens are diluted…

---

[67] "Foods for Cancer Prevention," Physicians Committee for Responsible Medicine https://www.pcrm.org/health/cancer-resources/diet-cancer/facts/foods-for-cancer-prevention

Also, bacteria in the colon ferment the fiber creating a more acidic environment which may make bile acids less toxic… Fiber is also protective against other forms of cancer…. Studies have shown that stomach cancer and breast cancer are less common on high-fiber diets."[68]

Another problem with meats, especially if they aren't organic, is the way in which animals are raised: in inhumane conditions of captivity, without seeing sunlight, while fed with GMO products like corn (when in fact many of these animals should be fed only with grass), and receiving constant administration of hormones to accelerate their growth. It isn't surprising that these poor animals suffer diseases and are constantly ingesting antibiotics. Obviously, when we eat these meats, we also ingest a portion of all these hormones and antibiotics because it has been left in the animal's body. These animals suffer from the moment when they are born until the moment they die. All of that negative energy is also passed onto our bodies when we consume them.

One of the things that most significantly caught my attention when I worked with kids and teenagers was

---

[68] Ibid.

how quickly they develop nowadays. Not terribly long ago, puberty used to start at around age fifteen, but currently, it can start around age eight or nine, and in extreme cases, even at age seven. In a study published by *Pediatrics* magazine, it states that, "The proportion of girls who had breast development at ages 7 and 8 years, particularly among white girls, is greater than that reported from studies of girls who were born 10 to 30 years earlier." [69]

Early development can relate to the emergence of depression, anxiety, premature sexual activity, dietary imbalances, weight problems, psychological disorders, and alcohol and drug use. The Scientific Committee on Veterinarian Measures related to Public Health (SCVPH) presented a report that says that among all of the hormones that are used in meat production, six of them (natural and artificial) are potentially harmful to humans who ingest them because residual hormones that remain in the meat could alter humans' endocrine balance. This could cause chronic health problems. [70]

---

[69] Frank M. Biro., Maida P. Galvez., Louise C. Greenspan., et al., "Pubertal assessment Method and Baseline Characteristics in a Mixed Longitudinal Study of Girls," Journal of Pediatrics, 126, (2010), 583-590

[70] "Growth Promoting Hormones Pose Health Risk to Consumers, Confirms EU Scientific Committee," European

These conclusions are based on the result of studies done on cows fed with grain so that they fatten up quicker than if they had been allowed to graze, and on other agricultural methods that involve the use of hormones in the breeding of animals.

In general, I try to eat meat twice per week, and when I do so I try to choose fish or white meat like chicken or turkey, after always making sure that they are organic, as these animals live a much better life and are fed naturally and without antibiotics. I do the same with dairy products like cheese and eggs. As I mentioned before, you don't have to eat organic products all the time, especially if they are expensive for you, but if there is something that you can invest in to improve your health through your diet, make sure that it is in the meat and dairy products that you consume. The possibility of a disease can end up costing you so much more than the money than you would spend buying organic products.

Dr. Klaus Stöhr, a scientist from the World Health Organization (WHO), informs us that, "the generalized use of antibiotics in agriculture and cattle poses serious

Commission. Press Release Database, April 23, 2002.http://europa.eu/rapid/press-release_IP-02-604_en.htm?locale=en

issues because some resistant bacteria that have recently emerged in animals are transmitted to humans, mainly through animal products or through direct contact with farm animals. Treating diseases caused by these resistant bacteria in people is harder and more expensive, and in some cases the available antibiotics are no longer efficient." [71] Similarly, an article published by the *Washington Post* notes some antibiotics used to treat diseases in people are also widely used in cattle to promote the prevention of diseases and weight gain, and to compensate for the overcrowded conditions of ranches and farms. The antibiotics are mixed in the animas' food, in low doses, for such long periods that the practice has begun producing "super-bugs" that are resistant to medications and that may spread to human beings who work with or eat these animals. [72]

While I educated myself more on protein sources, I learned that it wasn't necessary to consume meat all the time in order to get the protein that my body needs.

[71] Stohr, Klaus., "Resistencia a los Antimicrobianos. Problemas del Uso de Antimicrobianos en la Agricultura y la Ganadería," Boletín de Medicamentos Esenciales y Política Farmacéutica de la OMS, 28 y 29 (200), 10-12, http://apps.who.int/medicinedocs/pdf/s2250s/s2250s.pdf
[72] Kennedy, Donald., "The Threat From Antibiotic Use on the Farm," The Washington Post, August 23, 2013, washingtonpost.com https://goo.gl/44dU48

Therefore, I started incorporating proteins derived from plants into my diet. These are often much healthier because they don't contain cholesterol or fats, are digested better, and are rich in fiber. However, I am not advocating for a vegetarian or vegan diet because I think that each person should experiment with the nutrients that work best for his or her body and lifestyle. In my case, for example, I had to reduce red meat and stop drinking cow's milk because it caused me inflammation, gas, and intestinal discomfort. I often advise my clients that if they want to stop using a meat product, do so for a week and then see how they feel. If they notice improvement, then it has been a good choice for them, and we will add it to their diet plan. It is very personal and individual for each body though. My fifteen-year-old daughter stopped eating meat because she felt bad about the suffering and killing of animals. I reduced its intake for health issues. Whatever your preference is, make sure that it always contributes something positive to your general wellbeing.

I personally recommend following a balanced diet with animal and vegetable proteins. Among the protein sources that I personally like are fish caught in the wild and not raised in farms; legumes like chickpeas, black, and white peas, dried peas, and beans; and nuts like peanuts, almonds, pistachios, walnuts, and hazelnuts. Among the vegetables, I like spinach, portobello

213

mushrooms, cauliflower, broccoli, and kale. I would also like to add that one of the biggest benefits of eating fish is the intake of Omega-3 fat, which is essential for the brain and sight, aids in combating rheumatoid arthritis, asthma, lupus, liver disorders, cancer, is good for inflammation, and balances weight. We also find Omega-3 in seafood, tofu, almonds, nuts, nut and rapeseed oil, and flax oil. Aside from the benefits that I just mentioned, this particular type of fat helps maintain cardiovascular health as well. There are specialists who think that the acids present in Omega-3 also prevent the macular degeneration of the eye, a very common type of blindness, and have positive effects on the treatment of depression.

In a study conducted in collaboration by the Queen Sofia University Hospital, Lipids and Arteriosclerosis Unit, Córdoba University, Maimónides Institute of Research in Biomedicine in Córdoba (IMIBIC), Cyber Physiopathology Obesity and Nutrition, and the Carlos III Institute of Health in Spain, it was observed that the intake of Omega 3 ·produces a decrease in cardiovascular risk. This has inspired influential scientific societies like the American Heart Association (AHA) and the European Society of Cardiology to recommend its intake; as such, Omega-3 fatty acids have been included in their guidelines, although with different levels of evidence. It has been proven in the different clinical trials that Omega-3 fatty acids can reduce cardiac events, in addition to decreasing the progress of arteriosclerosis. [73]

Good fats? They do exist

In addition to eliminating all processed food and junk food, I also eliminated partially hydrogenated or trans fats. Then I started reducing saturated fats that came from animal products, like margarine, cream, ice cream, whole milk, and certain meats. Consuming a lot of saturated fats can increase "bad" cholesterol and decrease the "good" one. Cholesterol is a lipid necessary for your body to work properly. Our body naturally produces cholesterol, but it also comes from the food we eat, especially animal products. So, the combination of internal and external sources of cholesterol should theoretically create a balance of it in the body. A little cholesterol is good because it helps prevent heart diseases. As I mentioned earlier, however, Americans eat up to double the portion of meat recommended daily. This causes the level of bad cholesterol to increase, which heightens the risk of

---

[73] Garcia-Rios, Antonio., Meneses, Maria., Perez-Martinez, Pablo., et al., "Omega-3 y Enfermedades Cardiovascular: Más Allá de los Factores de Riesgo," Nutricion Clinica y Dietética Hospitalaria 29 (2009): 4-16

heart disease and cerebrovascular incidents. Another kind of fat that I also limited was vegetable oils, or Omega-6 fatty acids, because many of them, like canola or soy, contain GMOs and have been processed. To produce these kinds of oils, oil seeds are put through chemical treatments that make them lose all of their properties, including color, smell, taste, and the nutrients that are so beneficial for our bodies.

While I wrote this book, the United States finally decided to prohibit the use of trans fats. The U.S. Food and Drug Administration (FDA) announced on June 16 of 2015 that it is necessary to remove this ingredient from food because of the evidence that has been gathered about its harmful effects on human health. The agency said that, "were no longer "generally recognized as safe," or GRAS, for short… Now that partially hydrogenated oil is no longer generally recognized as safe, FDA is providing a three-year compliance period. This will allow industry to gradually phase out the remaining uses over a three-year period, or seek food additive approval for those uses." [74] Susan Mayne, director of the FDA Center for Dietary Health and Applied Nutrition said that, "We made this

---

[74] "FDA Cuts Trans Fat in Processed Foods." United States Food and Drug Administration, June 16, 2015. 1-2 fda.gov https://www.fda.gov/ForConsumers/ConsumerUpdates/ucm3729 15.htm

determination based on the available scientific evidence and the findings of expert panels... Studies show that diet and nutrition play a key role in preventing chronic health problems, such as cardiovascular disease, and today's action goes hand in hand with other FDA initiatives to improve the health of Americans." [75] The new rule will go into effect starting June 18th of 2018. That means that trans fats will still be on the market for a while, so in the meantime make sure that when you buy vegetable oil, it says 100% vegetable and organic.

While reducing bad fats, I also started adding natural fats like Omega 3, virgin olive oil, coconut oil, avocado oil, and some seeds like sunflower, pumpkin, and sesame oil that are beneficial for digestion, have anti-inflammatory properties, help maintain a healthy weight, and promote intestinal health, among other things. Coconut oil, for example, reinforces thyroid function, strengthens the immune system, and aids in the maintenance of young and healthy skin. Avocado oil prevents varicose veins and phlebitis, balances blood pressure, is good for skin regeneration, and delays the aging of the cells. Olive oil improves circulation, helps maintain youthful skin, reduces cholesterol, balances blood sugar levels, and is a powerful antioxidant.

---

[75] FDA Cuts Trans Fat in Processed Foods." p. 2

Something very interesting about olive oil is that it is an important component of the Mediterranean diet. People in this region of the world have lower risks of heart disease, high blood pressure, and cerebrovascular incidents compared to North Americans and Northern Europeans.

"Healthy and varied nutrition is key to preventing diseases, having energy to enjoy life, and feeling strong enough to overcome obstacles." – Author Unknown

Your own chef

After changing my diet, the next step was to start cooking at home. At the pace that we live, cooking at home is often difficult and rather uncommon for a lot of people. In addition, sometimes people feel it like an obligation rather than an enjoyable task. But even if you initially feel some fear or resistance in the kitchen (just like some of my clients who feared that the food was going to come out wrong), the truth is that it can be done with a lot of success. In the beginning, I also found cooking to be a bit challenging. Given that I was sick and had no energy, it was much more practical for me to put frozen food in the microwave. But because of my ailments, I knew that I had to cook my own food in order to heal. Furthermore, in the process of learning to love my body, I wanted to give it the right kinds of food, and cooking allowed me to control the ingredients and the quality of my meals, which simultaneously helped me to control my health. As the great American cook, Julia Child, said, "no one is born a great cook, one learns by doing."

To start, I began experimenting with different textures, smells, and flavors. I always tried to practice different recipes, especially with various herbs and ingredients that helped my healing, like turmeric (which is good for pain), ginger, basil, garlic, and different types of fruits and vegetables. It is nice to eat in restaurants occasionally, but when it becomes the rule rather than the exception, then it is possible that your body will start showing signs of unbalance, like eating disorders or weight gain. Needless to say, when you eat out, you don't know how the food was prepared, or where it came from, or how long it has been stored. There is nothing better than knowing what you are eating, and cooking is the only way to know exactly what you are putting in your stomach. There are several studies about the benefits of cooking at home. In one of them, conducted by the Johns Hopkins Bloomberg School of Public Health Research, the research team concluded that, "people who frequently cook meals at home eat healthier and consume fewer calories than those who cook less ... The findings also suggest that those who frequently cooked at home – six-to-seven nights a week

– also consumed fewer calories on the occasions when they ate out." [76]

Once I started cooking at home, not only did my health improve, which provided me with immense satisfaction, but it also brought me much closer to my family. When I was sick and not able to do it on my own, the girls helped me, and that became a social and collaborative moment for us. I taught my daughters to cook, and my husband also helped. We had a lot of fun preparing the food that we liked the most, then, once we tasted what we had worked to create, we enjoyed our food eve more. In addition, the various delicious aromas that we experimented with while we cooked helped us to have a healthy appetite because the sense of smell initiates the production of gastric juices that induce appetite. Now, my girls know how to distinguish healthy foods from unhealthy ones. This is also very good for kids nowadays, who are bombarded by advertisements that try to convince them that certain foods are good for

---

[76] "Study Suggests Home Cooking is a Main Ingredient in Healthier Diet," <u>John Hopkins Bloomberg School of Public Health: Center for a Livable Future</u>, November 17, 2014. Jhsph.edu <u>http://www.jhsph.edu/research/centers -and-institutes/johns-hopkins-center-for-a-livable-future/news-room/News-Releases/2014/Study-Suggests-Home-Cooking-Main-Ingredient-in-Healthier-Diet.html</u>

them, when in fact they are not.

Another advantage of eating at home is that the food is prepared with love and good energy because even it seems doesn't seem true, the love that you put into your food does affect it. In Asian cooking, for example, the mood and emotional state that the person is in while he or she cooks is very important. This culture believes that if someone is sad, in a bad mood, or depressed while he or she cooks, the person's negative energy is going to be transmitted into the food and then affect those who eat it.

A basic list of fresh foods that I always try to have in my refrigerator are:

- Vegetables

- Fruits

- Organic fish and poultry.

- Dried fruits, like nuts, almonds and peanuts, that are healthy alternatives to cookies or candies

- Olive oil

- Legumes

- Whole grains, like quinoa, whole grain flour, whole grain bread and pasta, brown rice, oatmeal, and whole grain cereals

- Natural sugars like honey or agave

- Fresh or dry herbs to season my food, like cilantro, oregano, basil, pepper, cinnamon, chili powder, curry powder, ginger, balsamic, rice or vanilla vinegar, etc.

- Himalayan Salt

- Almond butter or organic butter

- Almond, coconut, or organic soy milk

- Organic eggs

- Natural yogurt, neither flavored nor colored, because they may be artificial

- Green tea

- Raw chocolate

- Garlic

- Mustard

- And, of course, water.

"You don't have to cook fancy or complicated masterpieces, just good food from fresh ingredients." – Julia Child.

Healing the soul

I remember reading a phrase that said, "pay attention to your body." Sometimes it gets sick so that you can heal your soul. When you start loving your body, you also learn to heal your internal wounds. It doesn't matter how well you eat or exercise; healing starts on the inside. Nowadays we often try to heal from the outside while forgetting about our inner self. Doctor Edward Bach (1886- 1936), who was a British doctor, homeopath, bacteriologist, and spiritual writer, believed that the true causes of disease are: fear, ignorance, grief, impatience, mistakes, and doubt. These, if we allow them to, are reflected in our body, causing disease. By failing to understand the true causes, we have attributed our lack of harmony between the body and soul to external influences like germs, cold, or heat, and we have named the results arthritis, cancer, asthma, etc., as we wrongly believe that the disease starts in the physical body. [77]

As I mentioned before, there are people who, in order to address their depression, turn to drugs or food, but these only offer temporary relief. No food or negative habit is going to heal that pain that you have gone or are going through. In my case, I was aware that even if I ate well and exercised, I still had feelings of depression, low self-esteem, fear, and even some phobias. I realized that these feelings were a message from my body warning me that something wasn't quite right. I knew that I had to pay attention to these signs because otherwise, I was never going to achieve total wellbeing, and my healing would only ever be temporary.

I remember that once, while in church, the minister mentioned that the past should be contemplated with gratitude, the present considered wonderful, and the future regarded with hope. These words helped me a lot. The more I forgave and accepted myself, even with my "failures" and "flaws," the more my mind and body strengthened. I felt far more connected with my environment, and I was more social and open than I

---

[77] Bach, E. "Heal Thyself. An Explanation of the Real Cause and Cure of Disease." United Kingdom: The Bach Center. 2009 http://www.bachcentre.com/centre/download/heal_thy.pdf

had been up to that point. A deep sense of intimacy with all of creation started taking root in the place that was previously inhabited by my fears. I felt safe because deep down I knew that everything was going to be ok—that everything was ok. While I was still connected with the survival mechanism of my youth, I could simultaneously understand things better and use my empathy to liberate myself from the anger and resentment in order to finally taste forgiveness.

Like many of my clients, I was also raised by parents who hadn't learned to love themselves because nobody taught them. They hadn't lived the experience of feeling loved, or appreciated, or understood. Their parents probably didn't know how to do it either. They were the last link of a chain of victims of other victims, who had focused on survival and who somebody in the family had to cut themselves off from in order to stop the cycle from continuing. I decided to learn to love myself, even if no one had explained how I should do so. I also noticed that the more that I loved my body, the more my self esteem grew, which made me feel wonderful because I accepted myself just as I was, without caring about the way that I had been raised.

There is an affirmation of self-acceptance that I love, and I would like to share it with you, in the hopes that it helps you as much as it helped me. It is a group of phrases by Brené Brown that I compiled, and it would be good that, if you can, you read it every day because, as the saying goes, practice makes perfect. Here you have it:

"I am strong, I am weak, I am imperfect… I am broken, I am vulnerable, I am human. And despite all these flaws, I allow myself to love me unconditionally. I am growing, evolving, using my past mistakes as fuel for my journey. I accept myself as I am, and I give myself the intention of being the person I want to be."

This is another affirmation that I wrote, reminding myself of the importance of self love:

"It took me a while, but really learning to love myself was the best thing that I have done for me, my health, and my happiness. When I started to really love myself, I started to worry more about caring for my body and being happy and worrying less about others' approval, their drama, and negativity."

I know that it can be difficult for people to love themselves, but as Buddha says: "You yourself, as much as anybody in the entire universe deserve your love and affection."

Here I leave you with some advice that I offer to my

clients and use on myself to help value and love my
body:

- I focus on the moment.

- I appreciate my body as it is, with its "ups and
  downs."

- I recognize my defects and love them as parts
  of me. I don't complain about them.

- I value myself as a whole, knowing that my
  body isn't all but rather a part of myself, and
  there are also other important parts that aren't
  tangible, like my personality, my emotions, my
  spirituality, and my intelligence.

- I remind myself that I am special, like we all are.

- I don't compare myself to anyone. Each of us
  has our own path to walk. I'm not better or
  worse. I enjoy who I am, and I try not to envy
  or desire what I don't have.

- I feed myself well and exercise regularly.

- I have a social life.

- I don't complain about my body. I recognize that not every body is perfect.

- I am grateful for every part of my life.

- I recognize that I have weaknesses, but I also have many strengths.

- I am very proud of my achievements, and I try to learn from my mistakes.

"Happiness can only come from inside of you, and it is the result of your love. When you realize that no one else can make you happy and that happiness is the result of your own love, you´ll have begun the most important autonomous path of your life." – Don Miguel Ruiz

CHAPTER 5

Enjoy your Freedom

"As I walked out the door toward the gate that would lead to my freedom, I knew if I didn't leave my bitterness and hatred behind, I'd still be in prison." – Nelson Mandela

I´ve decided to open this last chapter with a quote by Nelson Mandela because it summarizes the complete contents of this book and has aided me as one of my guidelines during my journey to self-healing and complete wellbeing. Every time I repeat it, I remember that if I don't care for my mind and my emotions, recognizing them in the first place and then finding space in which to express them, and if I don't free myself from the psychological pains that may harass me, sooner or later my immune system will be negatively affected, and this, inevitably, will lead me back to my own prison. In this way, I run the risk of falling back into the calamity of diseases and discomfort and straying away from wellbeing, health, and happiness.

I am aware that there are, unfortunately, people who free themselves from their prisons and then fall back into them after some time. These people might feel that they have failed in their attempt and that all their willpower and the work that they put into this effort useless. In fact, it´s not that their efforts were pointless; it's just that when this relapse happens, they usually feel guilty and unfit, and, in most cases, they don't try again for fear of failing once more.

In my private consultations as a health coach, I have witnessed numerous cases where people come to me because they feel depressed, overwhelmed, and lacking faith. These people often achieve their desired weight loss, but after a few months, they return because they have regained those lost pounds and sometimes even more. They are overwhelmed by a deep sense of failure that blocks them internally from taking a step in any direction, and that usually pushes them to eat more. Furthermore, when I worked as a family therapist, I saw many cases involving women who had left their abusive husbands, and yet returned to those men after a few days or months. Additionally, people who have stopped using drugs and alcohol sometimes relapse in the future. Still others think that they had beaten depression or issues with low self-esteem, only to find themselves back in a difficult or oppressive situation that causes these problems to reemerge. In these cases, depression, food issues, and addictive behaviors usually fill the void caused by our thoughts.

Given that everything depends on the thoughts that we have, we tend to return to the prison that we have escaped from when we still haven't healed our minds, which forces us back into the circle of, "I think, I feel, and I act." But the truth is, it doesn't have to be like this. Remember that your current situation is a product of your thoughts and beliefs, and these can be modified. During my own healing process, I learned that one of the reasons that we fall back into the same mistakes is because we lack a "plan" to follow that allows us to maintain physical, mental, and spiritual balance. I have great confidence that if you put my PlanPluz into practice, you will have the tools to be able to liberate yourself from your sorrows and find the happiness that you so much deserve because the more you learn and take care of yourself, the more the union between your mind and body will grow, and it then becomes possible to maintain good health.

I know that being able to enjoy freedom can be harder for some people than for others, either because of external present circumstances in the environment in which they live, or because of the presence of persistent debilitating diseases, or simply because they can´t accept the idea of a better future, despite the situation that they find themselves in. It was necessary for me to develop a plan that not only gave me faith and trust in myself, but also helped me to enjoy my freedom so that I don't lock myself up in a vicious circle again. That is why I would like to share with you some of these tools that I regularly use myself and with my clients on a daily basis.

Every morning, I usually read affirmations that help to me focus during the day. I generally try to do it as soon as I wake up and after expressing gratitude for a new day. An affirmation consists of the repetition of a positive thought that has been previously deliberately chosen, as a way of embedding it in our hearts and minds so that it assists us in removing obstacles, fears, blockages, or any other kind of negative thought. In other words, the negative thought detoxes from your body when you replace it with a positive thought or affirmation. This also helps you to change the feelings that lead you to repeat unfavorable behaviors in your life and then changes the direction of your actions towards wellbeing and the experiences that you wish to live. Repetition is used because this is the natural learning process of the mind. When you repeatedly use affirmations, you cause a gradual transformation of your thoughts until your mind learns to think only things that benefit you. The affirmations that you use can be inspired by other people, such as authors or therapists, or you can write your own with words that are familiar, believable, and make sense to you.

You can start with simple words that create positive images in your mind, such as "I deserve to be happy," and "today I will focus on the positive."

So, here are my affirmations:

- I trust and have faith in God.

- I am very thankful for everything that I have: my family, my home, my health, my friends, and nature.

- My body is my temple: I love and take care of it.

- I make space in my life to feed my mind and my body with healthy food, exercise, relaxation, and appreciation.

- I am in charge of my happiness.

- I chose to forgive and forget those who have hurt me. I also choose to stay away from people or places that are no longer useful for me or don't make me happy.

- I chose to believe in myself and my dreams, without caring how unattainable others may think they are.

Detox your mind

Detoxing is not only for your body but also for your mind. For me, it is necessary to keep my mind free of thoughts that can disrupt my wellbeing. Regularly creating a mental detox keeps my head free of bad ideas, images, and people who disrupt and block me from moving through life's difficulties with balance. You may occasionally find yourself repeating the same thoughts, like "I can´t do this," "it´s not going to keep on working," "I don´t deserve it," "I´m going to fail," or "this can end at any minute, and I am afraid of going back to where I was before." With this type of attitude, it is possible to lose our ambition, motivation, and faith. If this happens to you, it would be a good idea to pay attention to the words that you repeat to yourself in your mind; if they are good, listen to them and don´t repress them, but if they are bad, keep them away!

Try to identify the reason why the bad thoughts have returned. This is the moment of mental detox that I mentioned. Maybe you still have feelings of guilt; or maybe there are people around you who, instead of helping you, are negatively affecting you; or maybe the places that you visit, a type of entertainment that you use, friends whom you decide to spend time with, literature and materials that you read and hear are eliciting negative thoughts. Even the nightly news is usually negative nowadays, which can also cause anxiety. The important thing is to recognize these clues and not let them beat you.

You have the power to turn these bad ideas into ones that benefit you. Make a list of what causes you bad feelings and check how you can fix and transform them without having to relapse. For example, instead of saying, "I'm going to fail," why not use, "I have the strength to change"? In this way, you begin to use the statements that will help you to change your mindset to positive thoughts. When faced with people who discourage you, substitute them with others who encourage you and help you to see the beauty of life. Instead of eating excessively or using any kind of drug because you feel depressed or anxious, go for a walk; sometimes being outdoors relaxes us and helps us to appreciate our lives in ways that nothing else can.

Focus on the positive

Nobody lives in an eternal state of happiness. It's impossible. We have to be realistic. We all have frustrations, anxieties, and setbacks. The fact that you repeat the same behavior that you wanted to change doesn't mean that you have lost the battle, nor does it define the kind of person you are. When these things happen, it's not the time to judge yourself. In the same way that you have achieved success in the past, you can make the efforts to do so again. Next time something disappointing happens, take some time to see what went wrong, and analyze the situation so that you know how to deal with it better in the future. Remember that even these unfortunate events can turn into something good. Unfortunately, when setbacks happen, we tend to focus on negativity, fear, worries, and self-criticism instead of what can be learned from them.

Even if we can't control daily disappointments, we can control our thoughts. When you "auto-criticize," you are not looking for a solution; rather, you are fulfilling the victim role again. Each problem has a solution or a lesson, so focus on what you can solve. Try spending less time complaining and mourning. Remember the reasons why you started to change, your strengths, your limitations, your abilities. We´re all born with certain talents and purposes. If it´s necessary, talk to yourself. Every morning, you can think about something positive about yourself. Make a list of everything that´s positive in your life, and remember to tell yourself, "I´m strong. I made it before, and I can make it now, I´m aware that what is happening to me is something temporary, and only I can change it. We all have problems; I´m not the only one. This is normal."

Maintain your optimism, recognize your abilities, and honor your achievements. Don't compare yourself to other people. Each person is fighting his or her own battle, and the fact that another person has been able to overcome his or hers without relapsing is no reason for you to get discouraged. You can achieve what you desire for yourself.

Do volunteer work

There is a quote that says that helping others can be the cure—not only for those in need, but for your soul as well. Indeed, doing volunteer work is good for your mental health. One thing that I´ve noticed is that volunteer work has, on several occasions, helped me to fight depression. It makes me feel more fulfilled and satisfied while also helping me to combat stress. It also allows me to maintain regular contact with others, which helps me to develop a much more solid support system and meet other people with values similar to mine. There are thousands of organizations with different types of volunteer work. All that matters is that you find something that you enjoy and can do.

Smile, smile

When I say smile, I don´t mean that you should be in a good mood all the time… even though that would be wonderful, I also know that it is impossible. However, being in a good mood can sometimes calm our fears and help us to express our negative feelings without causing us so much stress. I remember once I went to a comedy show where one of the comedians used his childhood traumas in a way that caused both he and the audience to laugh. He mentioned that humor allowed him to express his emotions honestly, which helped him to overcome any doubt or sadness. Laughter really can be good medicine.

When was the last time you smiled? What things make you smile? Whatever they are, start doing them more often. When you smile, you have fun. Fun and laughter are a balm that combats stress, strengthens the immune system, and helps our bodies to heal. Laughter is healing, and it also has the power to relieve depression, lower blood pressure, and relax us.

"Although no one can go back and make a brand new start, anyone can start from now and make a brand new ending." – Unknown author.

I want to end this book by reminding you about the importance of self-love. When we love ourselves, we are able to forgive, fight, and transform all of our positive and negative experiences into lessons. This quote by Charlie Chaplin is a beautiful reflection of how important it is to have self-love:

"As I began to love myself I freed myself of anything that is no good for my health – food, people, things, situations, and everything the drew me down and away from myself. At first I called this attitude a healthy egoism. Today I know it is "LOVE OF ONESELF."

In case it´s happening to you...

Each person is different, but many times we can identify with certain situations that will allow us to connect with other people's stories and to recognize our own conditions. In the following section, I will share with you some examples of cases that I´ve treated, wherein you may find some aspect that is familiar to you in some way or another. I´ve used fictional names to protect my clients' identities.

Case 1: Devaluation

Meredith is a 24-year-old woman—an only daughter who lives with her parents. When she came to see me, she suffered from depression, negativity, and hopelessness. She yearned to feel better and to lose her excess weight. She had followed several diets with difficulty and failed to achieve the desired results. She believed that she couldn't lose weight in any way because it was an inherited trait from her mother. So, she easily quit any attempt, blaming her parents for feeding her food "that makes you fat," for they were the ones in charge of the family meals. Meredith didn't cook, making excuses for herself because she found it "hard," and she'd rather eat the meals that her parents provided, which consisted mainly of fast food to takeout from restaurants. She had also dropped out of college because it was difficult for her, and she didn't know what she wanted to do with her life. She lacked decisiveness, blaming other people for her "failures" and always craving others' attention. Her dream was to become an actress, but without feeling comfortable with her body, she thought that she would never be considered for any role, so it was better "not to try." She compensated for her anguish by having casual sex with men she met online. She claimed that she'd rather have this kind of relationships because she believed that no one was going to fall in love with her, so in this way she avoided going through the pain of loving without being loved. Growing up without siblings and having always being prone to illness, she was used to having all of her parents' attention. In fact, her mother even paid for her consultations with me. Meredith was convinced that she could do nothing for herself, and even when she tried, the results did not meet her expectations.

Our plan was to make her aware of the areas that she should focus on in order to start taking responsibility for her behavior and then take the necessary steps to change it. As a first measure, she had to learn that she could only control her own behavior and not others' (she had to learn, for example, that even if she had no control over what her parents brought to the table, she could choose not to eat it). We started studying her thoughts and identifying their roots, then recognizing the causes of her negative behavior. We also focused on the appreciation of everything good that life had blessed her with, including parents who loved her and took care of her. We slowly broadened the focus towards the importance of her body and love for herself, aiming to stop engaging in confusing and risky sexual encounters and to start pursuing opportunities for a healthy and stable monogamous relationship where she could feel respected and valued. Gradually, Meredith would have to work on no longer allowing her past to control her present and future, seeking peace with things that disturbed her, and allowing herself to move on from those issues.

Finally, we looked for exercises that helped her to realize her value as an individual, for herself and for society in general, because we all have a unique gift to offer in this life, and thus we are all important. With time, she started to lose weight, and by setting simple goals, she started to achieve them while also training herself to face those that were more complex. She met a boy whom she liked, and she is finally in a stable relationship. She also signed up for an acting workshop, all of which made her very happy.

Case 2: Stress

Beatriz is a 45-year-old successful professional, who is single and has no family. She dedicated her entire life to a job that kept her busy for an average of 14 to 16 hours daily. With no time to take care of herself or sustain social activities, she found that her personal life had always been plagued by frustration. She told me that she preferred solitude because she didn't like to be criticized or judged, even though self-criticism, self-condemnation, and excessive perfectionism were prominent parts of her life. Growing up in a typical family with both parents and a sister, Beatriz had been compared to her sister ever since she was little— to the point that there were times when their parents made the girls compete for attention, then awarded "the winner" and neglected "the loser."

She had always fought to win her parents' love, but they also criticized all of her friends, boyfriends, and her social environment in general. She complained that she was overweight because of the long work hours, lack of rest, and her busy lifestyle that didn't enable her to have pleasant and healthy existence. She wanted to lose 25 pounds. Despite having tried a number of diets, she told me that she had always had problems with her weight. Like in many other cases, every time she lost weight on some super-restrictive diet, she would then abandon the regime and gain the weight back a short time later. Her diet consisted mostly of fast food that she ate between work meetings. She had gotten to the point that her health had started to be affected, as she suffered from swollen feet, backaches, fatigue, stomach aches, and difficulty concentrating. Medical evaluations found no disease that matched these symptoms, and the final diagnosis was stress.

When I asked her if she made any effort to relax, she said that she did, but that it didn't work. She also told me that she drank coffee and ate candies to keep her energy up and that one of the methods that she used to disconnect herself was to eat ice-cream and watch TV at night when she got home. She then usually started working again before going to sleep for four to five hours—sleep that was interrupted by anxiety about her workload. Upon evaluating Beatriz´s whole story, we started working on the awareness that her life reflected the ideas and thoughts of perfection that had been unconsciously imposed upon her by her parents.

Beatriz was trying to fit whatever idea of perfection she had. For this reason, she hid in loneliness so that no one could criticize her "imperfections," and she could avoid the rejection that she thought that she would suffer as consequence of those faults. A new idea emerged in her sessions: nobody can be perfect; this is a fantasy that is impossible to achieve because we all make mistakes and learn from them. These words may seem obvious to many people, but for someone who is a perfectionist, such sentiments are very hard to listen to and even more difficult to adopt.

We focused on her understanding of where this idea of perfection came from and on efforts to start letting it go in order to make way for an acceptance of all parts of herself, even those that she found "imperfect." We made a list of all of her personal achievements for her to have on hand so that she could read and remember frequently, highlighting the positive and decreasing the attention that she gave to the negative. I also helped her to understand the nutritional value of foods and to modify her diet with food that was healthy and came from Mother Earth. In this way, she started transforming herself by replacing her diet with organic, natural, and homemade meals (I taught her how to cook some easy, tasty, and healthy meals). To ease the stress, I advised her to engage in some activity that caused her pleasure and joy. She enrolled in a dance class, which she had always liked to do, and this immediately improved her wellbeing.

When Beatriz was ready, she signed up with an excursions group on the weekends, which allowed her to start socializing while also increasing her physical exercise and connecting with nature. As a result of our therapy, her stress level decreased significantly. Her sleep became more restful and increased to seven or eight hours daily because as her confidence grew, she started delegating work to other people, thus reducing her long work hours. Her energy levels rose naturally, and her life started to fill with joy and appreciation. Consequently, the overweight Beatriz disappeared, as she returned to a healthy weight for her body type. Beatriz lost the 25 pounds she wanted to lose, and she is currently working on maintenance.

Case 3: Overweight in adolescence

A 14-year-old and her mother came to see me for the teenager's weight issues. When they arrived, the mother expressed great concern about her daughter´s unhealthy weight, and she asked me to help her lose some. As always, we started the session listening to both women's problems and difficulties. While the mother tried to maintain a healthy routine, balancing an adequate diet with physical exercise, her daughter did the opposite, and all of the daughter's attempts to change went nowhere—she always fell back into junk food and a sedentary lifestyle. This was a cause of great disagreement between mother and daughter, creating mutual frustration. The mother complained that the daughter abandoned her efforts too quickly, despite all of the money that she spent in vain to find a solution. Meanwhile, the daughter blamed the mother for her bad habits, complaining that her mother always called her "fat, ugly and lazy." This also caused her a lot of sadness and made her seek comfort in sweets. Every time the two fought and the mother started insulting the girl, the girl looked to junk food to feel better and gain some power over herself because she felt that this was the only thing that she could control. On the other hand, the mother believed that she was helping her daughter try to avoid the emotional and physical suffering that obesity could cause her, specifying that "nobody was going to pay attention to her" if she remained at her current weight. It is worth mentioning that the mother had been overweight during her childhood, which made her the victim of verbal abuse and mockery from her family. Therefore, she went to great lengths to maintain her weight by dieting constantly, and using laxatives, pills, and exercise. The mother also felt guilty "for not being a good mother and not being able to help her daughter." To start, I began working with the mother, helping her to understand that her obsession with her daughter´s weight came from a painful past when she herself had suffered a lot for being "fat." We recognized her fears of obesity and the negative impact that those fears had on her relationship with her child.

One of the tools that I suggested for the mother was the use of a diary where she could dump her emotions and worries instead of unloading them on her child. Then we worked on the acceptance of her daughter, so she could learn to love her just as she is, without criticizing or embarrassing her. I also worked to educate her on how to maintain an ideal weight without diets or pills and helped her to be able to recognize the difference between the foods that help the body and those that don't. Afterwards we turned to the issue of her low self-esteem as a mother.

With the daughter, I worked on looking for alternatives to consuming food when she felt frustrated and sad. In addition, I had her write and share her feelings with her closest friends. To this program we added education about healthy foods, and the importance of leading a balanced life with physical exercise, rest, and fun. I also gave her some relaxation techniques to help her deal with her fear of being overweight.

With time, the mother's criticisms and insults decreased, and they both started to find a balance in their communication. The girl discovered new ways of talking with her mother and expressing herself in a more open way, using the words "I feel…" among other phrases. Once this communication issue was settled, she started to feel less frustrated with her life. She also enrolled in swim lessons, since that was what she liked to do, and took a yoga class with her mother. They both started cooking their meals at home. Consequently, the girl's weight gradually decreased. She has lost about 15 pounds now, and we are still working on it. Her mother enrolled in some group classes for parents of teenagers, which broadened her communication tools and decreased her guilt of being "a bad mother."

Case 4: Depression and Obesity

John is a 58-year-old widower and father of two sons who are 17 and 19 years old. His wife died of cancer ten years ago, and he came to see me because he was always tired, depressed, and about 45 pounds overweight, which led to cardiac problems and made his doctors advise him to modify his diet. His eldest son was already in college, and the younger one lived at home with him. John had tried to follow a vegetarian diet for a while without success, as it was very hard for him to stop eating meat, especially while sharing his meals with his teenage son, who had no interest in becoming a vegetarian. John had difficulties expressing his emotions and only wanted to talk about his weight. Until his wife´s death, John had never had problems with his weight, but he still grieved her passing, and ever since, he had lost all interest in himself and his looks, taking care only of his children.

The plan that we developed started by focusing on food—through education of healthier options like fish, nuts, olive oil, fruits, and vegetables, and in the reduction of fats that are harmful to our health. As John started trusting our efforts more and felt comfortable, we started working on a program of physical exercises (walking 30 minutes per day), relaxation techniques, and stress management. Little by little, he started understanding that the past can't be changed, that we should thank it for what it has taught us, and let it go with love, compassion, and forgiveness for the pain that we feel.

John told me that before his wife passed away, he enjoyed a lot of the meetings hosted by his church, but that afterwards, he was mad about what had happened, and he lost his faith and stopped attending, even though he missed his time there. So, gradually, I helped him to understand that his feelings and thoughts were contributing to his depression and affecting his lack of social interaction. When he understood this, he made the decision to return to church, which significantly helped him to overcome his loneliness. His cardiac health improved because of his diet and lifestyle changes, and he began trusting more and sharing his feelings in our sessions. In this way, he was able to vent the emotions that had imprisoned him for years. I then recommended him to a support group for people who had lost a loved one because he was ready to let go of all of that pain. Finally, in time, John decided to pursue his passion for tennis, which gave him joy.

I leave you with a quote for reflection: "There is a vitality, a life force, an energy, a quickening that is translated through you into action, and because there is only one of you in all of time, this expression is unique. And if you block it, it will never exist through any other medium and it will be lost. The world will not have it."
– Martha Graham

ANEX 2

PRISONERS

Marilyn Monroe: Not everything that shines...

I still remember the first time that I heard the name "Marilyn Monroe." It came out of my father's lips while he admired her picture and made comments about her unparalleled beauty, regretting that such a beautiful woman had died in such a tragic and sudden way. In that moment I didn't know about the circumstances of her death, nor did I know who she was...

I later learned that she was an American actress, model, and singer who passed away in 1962, at the age of 36, of a barbiturates overdose. Until that moment, I had never heard my father talk about beauty, especially in reference to a woman, and that included my sister and me. He had never said things like, "what a beautiful daughter I have" or "how pretty my girl looks today." When I got closer to see the image of Marilyn, I could see her beauty for myself, but at the same I felt a lot of uncertainty. I looked nothing like that fascinating woman who was apparently worthy of my father's admiration. I didn't have her eye color, nor her perfect hair, nor her pale skin. I had no way to dress in her style of clothes and shoes. There was nothing in the world that could have allowed me to be like her, and so I was not beautiful. When I look back, I can see that this was a significant moment in the beginning of my struggle with depression and low self-esteem that then burrowed deeper within me as time passed.

I pictured Marilyn very happy, surrounded by friends and love. I also envied her a little because I would never have what she had: beauty, money, fame, happiness, a perfect life. I thought of how nice it would be to have such grandeur and bliss—to have everybody admire and love you and want to be you. How would that feel? I pictured myself like that, feeling so happy, doing any and everything that I could think of, having my closet full of the latest fashions, surrounded by fans and people who love me, living in a big house where I would throw parties every weekend and invite all my friends to dance and have fun. I would never be alone again! I remember once when I saw her in a picture with her husband, Joe DiMaggio. They were about to get on a plane, and she looked so happy and sure of herself. I imagined her having a perfect marriage, after having grown up in a united family, where her parents loved her for being a beautiful and charismatic girl. How I would´ve liked to be Marilyn Monroe! It was in the United States that I finally learned more about Marilyn´s personal life. I couldn't believe when I read that, in actuality, she always felt alone and was very insecure. I would´ve never imagined how much that woman suffered and how unhappy her life was.

Marilyn was the third daughter of a mother who had psychological problems and a father whom she had never met. Her mother couldn't raise her, and the girl grew up in foster homes. Even if her mother came to get her daughter out of the foster care system, she was admitted in a psychiatric hospital shortly thereafter. Marilyn was then left in the care of the state until she fell back into a series of foster homes.

The envy that I initially felt for her soon became admiration. She had come so far, despite having been raised poor, with no family love or education. She had accomplished so much, and done so all alone, through her own strength and conviction. I imagine that this woman had to fight a lot to get to the place that she was in. Unfortunately, despite her achievements, she lived a very unhappy life. Her beauty and the confidence that she presented before the press hid a person who was actually extremely depressed and insecure.

She also suffered in love. Despite being one of the most desired women in history, she was married three times, and each marriage ended in a horrible divorce. She once said, "I'm trying to find myself as a person, sometimes that's not easy to do. Millions of people live their entire lives without finding themselves. But it is something I must do." I wondered why a person who, in my opinion, had it all (wealth, beauty, fame) wasn't happy. Unfortunately, Marilyn never overcame her past. Even if her professional life flourished, with incomparable international success and recognition, her personal life sank at the same speed, into alcohol, loneliness, depression, low self-esteem, and every kind pill that might ease her anxiety and help her to sleep. This woman fought alone, her whole life, against the obstacles that ultimately beat her. From her, I learned that external beauty is nothing if you are not happy inside as well.

"A sad soul can kill you quicker, far quicker, than a germ." – John Steinbeck

Robin Williams: In his own "cage"

I knew this actor/comedian's work when I arrived to the United States. I had been delighted with him ever since I saw the movie "Mrs. Doubtfire," a comedy in which he plays a father of three children who, after getting a divorce and losing custody of his kids, decides to dress up as a woman to work as his kids' babysitter and his ex-wife's housekeeper. This father takes great risks and undergoes a very significant change in his life to be able to be close to his children. When I saw the movie, I was very touched seeing the unconditional love that the character felt for his kids, and I admired the way that he treated them, with sweetness and respect. How I would´ve liked to have a relationship like that with my own father! Seeing it reflected in that story, I also felt hope that it is possible for parents to feel and demonstrate that unconditional love towards their children, and this taught me many things that I then experienced when I became a mother.

Another movie that I liked a lot was "Good Will Hunting," a drama in which Robin plays a psychologist who helps a young janitor with an unmatched genius for mathematics to find a purpose in his life. The relationship between them reminded me of what I had had with my advisor in high school, who also helped me to forge a path for my life. I also identified with Robin´s character, for I too wanted to help people find themselves.

In 2014, when I heard the news of his death by suicide at age 63, I was shocked and filled with sadness. I couldn't believe that someone so beloved by audiences – someone who had made so many people laugh— could have been so unhappy that he felt that he had to take his own life. I immediately remembered a movie called "The Birdcage," which I saw in 1996. At that time, I was about to graduate from college, and even if I felt happy about finishing this chapter in my life, it was a period full of anxiety and confusion. The moment that I had waited for after such a long period of immersing myself in my studies was finally before me. But I wondered, "what now?" Thousands of fears about my future and my abilities overwhelmed me. I wondered if after all of the struggle, I was going to fail— if maybe I had thought that I was much better than I really was. The thought that I was "good for nothing" was again alive in my mind and heart.

I remember that I was buying my graduation dress, while consumed by worries, when I saw a movie theater. They were playing "The Birdcage," and without thinking much of it, I went to see the movie. Friends had told me that it was a lot of fun, and since I needed distraction, I decided to watch it. I also felt like laughing a little because I was always so busy working and studying that I hadn't smiled in ages. In this comedy, Robin plays the gay owner of a cabaret who, along with a drag queen couple, creates a complete sham so that his son (the product of a heterosexual affair) can introduce them as a normal, traditional, Christian family (instead of a gay Jewish family) to the conservative parents of his future wife. This movie is one of the few that has made me laugh more in my life than most things, and it was the first one that I had watched in which the main characters were homosexuals. Again, I connected with Robin's humility as he represented a father who makes the impossible happen in service of the love that he has for his son—to the point of even denying his own identity and pretending to be heterosexual in order to not be judged as being different and saving his son's relationship with his future in-laws. Even if the topic is very deep, the way in which Robin played it was fun, and through his sense of humor, he made me understand a lot of aspects about human beings. This is why it is one of my favorite comedies of all time. When I saw it, I couldn't stop laughing, and when it ended, I kept on laughing. It helped me a lot in that moment of immense stress and anxiety to forget my worries.

When I came out of the movie theater, I felt much

more relaxed. How I would have loved being near Robin all the time! Imagine how happy I would've felt being his friend, listening to his jokes and encouraging words, sharing his love for human beings and animals. From that moment on, I became a huge fan of this brilliant man, and even today, when I feel sad, I recall scenes from "The Birdcage" and my mood shifts. This is something that I will always thank Robin Williams for: all of the moments of happiness that he gave me. I am so sorry that I couldn't be of any help to him in his most difficult times—that I could not provide the encouragement that he needed in the same way that he did for me and millions of viewers around the world.

It is deeply saddening that the beloved Robin Williams couldn't free himself from his own past when he has helped so many people to regain their hope and happiness. According to his wife, Susan Schneider, Robin fought against depression, alcoholism, drugs, and anxiety for a long time. In an interview that he gave to Spanish version of *People* magazine, the actor commented that in his childhood, children were to be seen but not heard. In an interview on "Inside the Actors Studio" (2001), he mentioned that his mother was an important influence in the development of his sense of humor because he tried to get her attention and make her laugh. In other media opportunities, he described himself as a short, "chubby" kid, which also negatively influenced his social life. This, combined with the absence of his parents and their constant moves, turned him into a shy and lonely child. When I heard this, I had a hard time believing that this man who made us laugh, who delivered happiness to millions of people, could have had an unhappy childhood.

Even though my childhood was very different from Robin´s, I identified with his loneliness and sadness. I also couldn't express myself without being silenced or accused, and I was also shy and lonesome. I also felt what it meant to be seen but not heard. Even when you know that they see you, you feel invisible. These thoughts and feelings, even if they are sometimes subdued, chase us day to day. They may quiet themselves temporarily, but they are always there, ready to attack us when we least expect it. For example, when we feel happy, or we have achieved something that has cost us a lot of time and effort, these hidden pains can keep growing, even if we don't realize it. They grow so much that a time comes when we can´t stand them, and it is almost impossible for us to run away from them. I imagine that for Robin Williams, this internal suffering was his prison.

Despite his personal struggles, I still receive inspiration from his movies and his quotes. In fact, one that has always helped me and lifted my spirits is from "The Dead Poets Society":

"Carpe Diem. Seize the day. Make your lives extraordinary."

Whitney Houston: "Habits" that silenced a great voice

I started to really admire this famous African American singer, actress, and model after seeing the movie "The Bodyguard," in which she made her film debut in 1992. Despite having listened to her songs, I soon found that the one that was the most touching for me was "I Will Always Love You," which is still one of the most famous worldwide. Out of pure coincidence, at that time I was taking an African American studies class at college, and one of my assignments was to choose a famous African American individual and research his or her life and work. As I had been so impressed by Whitney´s voice in that song, I chose her for my assignment. Truly, when I watched the film, I was also fascinated by this woman's beauty. Deep inside, I felt good, and it gave me a lot of joy to see that a person who had the same skin color as me was celebrated for her beauty and her talent. Usually, in both Hispanic and American television, Caucasian woman are famous and recognized for their beauty and talent. I was raised watching soup operas, and I usually could never relate to any of the main characters because they were all white, beautiful, and highly gifted, while black women usually played the maids or the villains in the series. Such casting on television prevails even now, and it can lower the self-esteem of many people, especially teenagers who don't see themselves reflected in the public figures that appear on screen. I believe that it´s important that the characters, both males and females of all skin colors, are recognized and admired.

During my study on Whitney Houston, there were moments when, while listening to her sing, I closed my eyes and imagined that, in some way, I could share her voice. How nice it would feel to be able to sing in church like she had. I remember that I couldn't stop singing "I Will Always Love You." Ever since I was little, I had wanted to participate in the church choir, but my voice wasn't as good as I wanted, and I was afraid that people would make fun of me, so I decided not to do it. I also thought that maybe my life would´ve been easier if I had been as pretty as Whitney.

My love and admiration inspired me to choose Whitney again, this time when I mention her in this book. Although the first time that I wrote about her, I did it with a lot of joy, today I do it with a lot of sorrow after her death at the age of 48 due to a cocaine overdose. According to the press, her drug addiction and her suffering started after marrying Bobby Brown in 1992. Other sources, however, mention her addiction problems prior to her relationship with Brown. Whitney herself, in an interview with Oprah Winfrey in

2009, publicly stated that, "[my husband] was my drug," that her marital relationship was compromised by drugs and domestic abuse, and that it was "emotionally abusive." In fact, on several occasions, she explained that she stayed with Brown because of the "habit" that had become a part of her life, and that she had hope that everything would be better in time.

It might be very easy to judge the singer. I also wondered several times how it was possible that such a beautiful and talented person could endure so much abuse. Generally, abused women stay with their husbands because of economic or social dependence, but in Whitney´s case, neither money nor social position was a part of the problem. The truth is, you can't judge anyone. Each one of us is free to make our own choices in life, and oftentimes it is difficult to understand the choices that people make because we don't know the deep and personal histories that lead people to those decisions. The singer and actress Barbra Streisand publicly stated, "how sad her gifts could not bring her the same happiness they brought us." Apparently, the star also suffered from low self-esteem, which I never would have imagined given her talent and beauty, and this led her to bear the abuse and seek solace in cocaine.

In my work, I have dealt with a lot of women who have

been or continue to be victims of domestic violence. Many of them turn to drugs and alcohol to overcome the physical and mental anguish that the abuse causes them, and (similar to Whitney) they have often suffered in silence far more than close family and friends could imagine. Unfortunately, these women stay with their husbands in large part because of their low self-esteem, which tells them that they don't deserve to be loved or respected, that no one will love them, or that they don't have the luck of other women who are respected because they are worthier, etc. In many cases, they justify the beatings to themselves, thinking that it is what they deserve. In Whitney Houston´s case, after divorcing Brown, she tried several rehabilitation centers, but unfortunately, after her discharge, she relapsed into drug abuse. I want to close this section with something that Whitney said: "The biggest devil is me. I'm either my best friend or my worst enemy."

To her "best friend," I would like to thank that wonderful voice, which, through her songs, has given me courage during many difficult times in my life, especially the son "Step by Step," which I listen to almost every day because of her motivational and spiritual lyrics, "don't give up, you got to keep on moving on don't stop. I know you're hurting, and I know you're blue, I know you're hurting but don't let the bad things get to you. I'm taking it step by step, bit by bit, stone by stone, brick by brick, step by step, day by day, mile by mile, go your own way." This song fills me with inspiration, and when I have problems, it helps me to lift my spirit above them.

I would like to tell her "worst enemy" that it was a huge sadness that she sank Whitney into a prison from which she couldn't liberate herself, and which caused her death, leaving a deep hole in the hearts of her fans and admirers. Many artists spoke of their admiration for Whitney, but the one statement that surprised me the most was Madonna´s because she expressed practically the same feelings that I had for Whitney when she stated in the British newspaper, *The Sun*, that "one thing I was struck by with Whitney Houston is I remember she sort of came out as a singer around the same time I did… I remember looking at her singing and hearing people talk about her, and just thinking, 'Oh my God. She's such a beautiful woman and my God, what an incredible voice. I wish I could sing like that… I just remember being extremely envious of her and also touched by her innocence."

Michael Jackson: A cry in loneliness

The death of the 51-year-old musician, actor, composer, and dancer due to a lethal dose of Propofol, a powerful anesthetic, fatally mixed with other medicines to treat insomnia and anxiety, shocked me immensely. Since the time when I was little, back in La Romana, I have listened to and admired Michael, and I would've never thought that such a famous, wealthy, and globally admired person would have problems with sleep or suffer from anxiety. It´s an important paradox because this musician gave so much relief and help to countless people, yet suffered so much himself. I remember as if it was yesterday when his album, "Beat It," was released. I was nine and fascinated by his music, his charisma, and his way of dancing. And because I´ve always liked dancing, I loved copying his moves. I simply adored the way that he let the music flow through his body, the freedom I felt when I saw him dance, and his inviting voice. Even if I didn't have a clue what the song was about, I felt an impulse to sing. Through him, I realized the power of music to gather people across cultural, racial, language, and religious barriers. Human beings are always willing to answer to music; it's like a language that comes from the heart, joining us through dance, singing, or simply by listening to it together.

In my neighborhood, for example, no kid understood what the songs said, and yet we all gathered in the streets, competing with each other to see who danced the most like Michael. This became so common that the people in the neighborhood decided to close the streets and create a friendly competition that included people of all ages to see who was Michael´s best imitator. The singer, without knowing, united the whole neighborhood! I remember that day everybody was happy, and both adults and children participated in the competition. That moment was one of the few happy moments of my childhood. To date, his music has the same effect on me. I didn't win the competition, but it was amazing to see the whole neighborhood happy for a while, including my family. That afternoon, nobody was sad, or angry, or worried; there was only laughter and wellbeing. In that moment, I realized how music can uplift people´s spirits. It´s no coincidence that music therapy is used to heal diseases of the body and mind. Listening to Michael Jackson, I felt how the story of his songs and the rhythm of his music had the power to influence my mood, and I thought about the great responsibility that singers and musicians in general have, especially those who are as famous as Michael Jackson.

Even if his career was very controversial, between the esthetic surgeries, an unclear sexuality, and the accusations of child molestation, I can't judge him; I can only thank him for the joy that he brought to my life. If I could, I would like to tell him how much I admire his philanthropic activities, which, through his organizations, continue to help a countless number of people. Michael created the Heal the World Foundation, a charity organization that took low-income children to Jackson's ranch, where they were fed and cared for, and where they could play in his personal theme park and participate in other games that the singer had created to bring them joy. The organization also sends money to children and families worldwide who live in unsanitary conditions riddled with sickness, poverty, and war. In several of his songs, Michael used his music and lyrics to defend those who had been or were victims of abuse, like in "They Don't Care About Us" and "Little Susie," thus allowing him to speak about these issues to a very large audience.

For me, it would be wonderful to be able to do even a little percentage of the work that Michael did for the wellbeing of people and the planet, both locally and globally. It's hard for me to acknowledge that even if Michael Jackson had gained a privileged place in show business—one that he held for decades— through talent and hard work, he still couldn't escape his prison. It's very difficult to understand.

Michael lacked a normal childhood because he started working with his brothers as early as age seven to help support his family. In an interview with Oprah Winfrey, he confessed that during his childhood and adolescence, he felt alone and isolated. He said: "There were times when I had great times with my brothers, pillow fights and things, but I used to always cry from loneliness." He went onto explain, "People wonder why I always have children around. It's because I find the thing that I never had through them. Disneyland, amusement parks, arcade games — I adore all that stuff because when I was little, it was always work, work, work." He was born in a low-income African American family and lived with his parents and eight siblings in a two-bedroom house. From the time when he was little, he was beaten by his father, with whom he had a complicated relationship. I understand this perfectly, and if I could sit down with that little Michael, I would hug him and comfort him, sharing with him my own experiences of abuse so that he wouldn't feel so lonely. There are times when only a beaten kid can help other with the same problem… at least in understanding.

Elvis Presley: The king of excesses

My admiration of Elvis was born many years ago without me even knowing it. It turns out that when I was a girl, I loved a Christian hymn that is still one of my favorites today. It moves and inspires me every time I hear it and even more so when I sing it. I listen to it often during my morning walks, and it immediately connects me with God, filling me with peace, lifting my spirit (especially when I am outdoors), and bringing me sweet memories of my childhood at church. It's called "How Great Thou Art," and I would like to share with you some of its lyrics: "Oh Lord my God when I in awesome wonder consider all the worlds thy hands have made, I see the stars, I hear the rolling thunder, thy power throughout the universe displayed… Then sings my soul my savior God to thee how great thou art, how great thou art…"

I remember the first time that I went to a church in the United States, someone asked me what my favorite Christian song was, and I answered "How Great Thou Art." Then they asked me if I had ever listened to Elvis Presley sing it in English. The truth is, I wasn't familiar with his songs, movies, or personal life. When I decided to listen to his version of the hymn, I was stunned. His voice was amazing and hearing him sing my favorite hymn moved me much more than usual. I was so impressed. I had never thought that Elvis Presley sang Christian music, let alone that he won one of his Grammys for this album. So this is how I continued hearing my favorite hymn over and over again, sung by Elvis, until I memorized it completely in English.

When I read more about his life, I was saddened. Elvis was a singer, composer, and actor who had died in 1977, at the age of 42, due to a heart attack caused by a pharmaceuticals overdose. The autopsy done revealed a massive excess of barbiturates, sleeping pills, stress medicines, anti-depressives, etc., in his system.

In her book, Elvis and Me, Elvis's ex-wife, Priscilla Presley, writes that in 1962, the artist suffered from severe insomnia, and the doses of sleeping pills that he took were growing exponentially. These were combined with other medicines that helped counteract the side effects of the sleeping pills. Priscilla also commented that Elvis's problems magnified due to the prescription medicines that he took. I identified greatly with this struggle because when I got sick, I was also a prisoner of prescribed medicines that mixed together—including one to relieve the side effects of others. When you least expect it, without realizing, you can find yourself taking an excessive number of pills, and you don't even know what each one is for. I can understand how this leads to a dangerous and toxic physical state.

On one occasion, the singer said, "the image is one thing, and the human being is other. It´s very hard to live up to an image." Even those among us who society deems the greats struggle. Even if during his last years Elvis was overweight, abused alcohol and medication, and could barely make it to public appearances, this man was so blessed with an incredible voice and spread so much happiness and joy among his fans that his magic lives on to this day.

I want to close this section with the lyrics of one of Elvis's songs that I like a lot, "If I Can Dream": "if I can dream of a warmer sun where hope keeps shining on everyone, tell me why, oh why, oh why won't that sun appear. We're lost in a cloud with too much rain. We're trapped in a world that's troubled with pain. But as long as a man has the strength to dream, he can redeem his soul and fly…"

Unfortunately, the list goes on, with many other people who maybe aren't as talented or as famous, or perhaps even publicly known, but who have influenced your life in some way with their difficulties or tragic departures. It's good to keep in mind that despite all of this sadness, not everything is lost, and there is much hope for positive changes in our experience as human beings.

"Don´t let your past, whatever it is, darken your vision of a bright future." – Alex Rovira

ANNEX 3

LIBERATED

Oprah Winfrey: The power of attitude

This great woman has taught me—and continues to do so every time I think of her and her achievements—that it isn't your circumstances but rather your will and the attitude that you take towards life that determines how far you are able to go. Oprah is known for "The Oprah Winfrey Show," the most successful talk show in the United States, and possibly in history. Even if I wasn't raised watching her shows, the appreciation that I feel for this TV presenter, actress, producer, and philanthropist is embedded deep within my heart.

The first time that I heard about Oprah was in 1993 when I saw on the news that president Bill Clinton had signed a law called The National Child Protection Act, or the Oprah Bill. Having been an eloquent advocate of the legislation, Oprah was invited by the president himself to speak during the presentation ceremony. This law ensures parents that children won't be under the care of criminals. Some of the highlights of this law include: the establishment of a database of those convicted of child abuse and sexual crimes, drug crimes, etc. It also allows the institutions that work with children, such as schools and daycares, to have access to the criminal database in order to check on all those who apply for jobs, and it requires that every act of child abuse be reported to the appropriate authorities. Oprah said: "A part of my mission in life now is to encourage every other child who has been abused to tell. You tell, and if they don't believe you, you keep telling. You tell everybody until somebody listens to you…I don't want another child to be afraid of saying, 'This is what happened to me."

My own experience made me very excited and simultaneously intrigued to know more about Oprah. Who was she— this woman who had taken on something so important, like giving voice to thousands of abused kids who had suffered in silence until this point? These kids are often silenced by their abusers with threats and violence. Many times, when they dare to talk, even their own families don't believe them. People know that these cases exist, but they never imagine that it could be happening to their own children. Through the law, Oprah was able to provide first and last names, pictures, and testimonies that have opened up the possibility of recovery for these kids. In taking action, she has also helped to rescue them from the darkness and terrifying loneliness that they languished in. Because of her courage, I decided to research her life and watch her TV show.

When I did, I was stunned to learn about how she grew up, and my admiration for her grew exponentially. Oprah was born dark skinned in a part of the country where that skin color was equated with sin. She was born into the extreme poverty of a black ghetto in Mississippi, among the most racist states in the United States at that time. In addition to not being white, Oprah had darker skin color than her neighbors, which subjected her to discrimination even from her own race. From the time when she was young, she lived with her maternal grandmother, while suffering physical, emotional, and sexual abuse. She has publicly stated that she was repeatedly raped starting when she was nine. After so much suffering, a teenaged Oprah escaped from her house when she was 13 and had a child at 14, but the baby passed away shorty after being born.

Despite such immense suffering, not only did she

become the wealthiest African American of the 20th century; she was also the only billionaire black woman in North America. Oprah is also considered the biggest black philanthropist in North America and one of the most influential women in the world.

Like many people, when I saw her show, I felt deeply inspired. I saw that Oprah listened sincerely and paid attention to people's problems. She shared with them from the heart, with empathy and without judgment. She befriended the audience so that they would trust her with real, credible topics and discussions. When Oprah listened to her audience, she was "normal," accessible to everybody without racial, social, or economic distinction. What surprised me the most was the way that she shared her own history, thus putting herself on the same level with the rest of the people who told their own stories. This gave me a lot of inspiration to perhaps, someday, tell my own story.

Some of the things that she mentioned about her life elicited great empathy within me: her half-brother had died of AIDS and her half-sister overdosed; she suffered immense abuse; she had extensive family problems, breakups, and dysfunctional people in her life; she battled weight gain and struggled in her personal life. There were times when if felt like Oprah was talking directly to me, understanding and advising me. This happened to me in messages that I gleaned from her show, like: "Anyone who has been verbally or physically abused will spend a great part of their life rebuilding their self-esteem," or "on many occasions, when I couldn't say no, I was afraid that if I did I was going to offend or hurt someone's feelings, and that person, in my mind, was going to be upset with me." This made me feel an important connection with Oprah, and as a result, I followed her as an example of improvement. Even today, she still inspires me. Hearing her talk about her problems and the way that she has dealt with them helped me to overcome mine. Knowing that she successfully escaped from the prison of poverty and abuse to become one of the most powerful and beloved leaders in the world encouraged me. In short, for me, Oprah's message is that it doesn't matter how difficult your past was; you can always put pain aside and seek your own happiness. I would like to share with you one of Oprah's quotes that inspired me the most: "The greatest discovery of all time is that a person can change his future by merely changing his attitude."

César Chávez: The force of race

This is a person with whom I feel particularly connected, from a social standpoint. My connection to this incredible human being began when I was in college at the State University of New York, New Paltz. During my second year of studies (1994), one of my classmates mentioned that she volunteered with the children of numerous agricultural workers in the area. She taught them to read and write, many times in their own homes because there were kids who didn't go to school. She also taught English because even if many of the children were born in the United States, they didn't speak the language. She also assisted with homework assigned to those who were enrolled in school. I remember that I was pretty amazed by this story because I had no idea that such problems existed so close to my college. Admittedly, I also didn't know that there were so many farms nearby.

Come to find out, the small town of New Paltz is situated approximately 80 miles north of New York City, in the Hudson Valley, a region where almost 18 percent of the land is dedicated to farming. The food grown in this region makes up a significant portion of the agricultural business, compared to any other zone this close to the city. Most of the farm workers who cultivate these lands are in Ulster County, to which New Paltz belongs. The work force is made up mainly of illegal immigrants from Mexico, Central America, or other Latin American nations, who travel from harvest to harvest. For example, during the winter they go to Florida, and in the summer and fall, they go to the Hudson Valley to harvest the vegetables and apples.

One day I decided to join my friend in order to find out more about this social situation and the work that she did. What I found caused me great sorrow: most of the kids and teenagers couldn't go to school because they had to help their parents with the harvests. Some of them where eight or nine years old, and they found it hard to finish their studies because they travelled with their families from one place to another and therefore didn't have the time to study. The whole family worked 11 to 12 hours daily non-stop, seven days per week. I felt even greater pain upon witnessing the way in which workers lived with their families in camps. I remember one of the families reminded me of my childhood: there were seven people sharing a single bedroom in a small cabin, where only one bathroom served several workers at the same time. I would've never imagined or believed it if somebody had told me that in the United States you could live like this… as you lived in La Romana.

That day I returned home with more questions than

answers: Why aren't there laws that protect these workers? Why do they live in subhuman conditions without anyone paying attention to their rights? Why are kids born in these families deprived basic education while having to go to work to supplement the very low income of their parents? I was outraged. These workers are the backbone of the country, and yet they weren't respected. The owners of the farms literally benefit on the backs of their labor and treat them worse than animals, with no regard for the sacredness of human life. I felt that the situation that I had just witnessed was exploitation—some kind of modern slavery. I was so bothered by the situation that I decided to sign up for training to become a union organizer in order to help these workers and give my humble contribution to social justice.

A union organizer provides workers with safe labor representation in their workplace, while also identifying those who aren't organized, informing them, helping them to develop leadership abilities, and organizing their union activities. I travelled to San Francisco, California, where the AFL-CIO offered a three-day course. It was here that I first learned of César Chávez, a Mexican-American agricultural worker, union leader, and civil rights activist who passed away in 1993 at the age of 66 after leaving a unique legacy of social justice, non-violent protest, and solidary action that still touches the lives of many individuals, including me.

And even if I thought that workers were still mistreated and living in unacceptable conditions, I learned that in Chávez's time, it was even worse: the farmers worked in subhuman conditions without being paid and without having the right to form unions, while most other American workers could. During the Great Depression, his family lost everything, and he was forced to travel to California to work in the fields, suffering countless difficulties of all kinds, mostly due to the constant poverty and the great physical work that they did during the year. Chávez had to quit school in seventh grade to take his mother's place in the fields because he didn't want her to continue working in them. With time, he began to realize that this kind of work was discriminatory and provided salaries far below the minimal income. In addition, he observed that workers and their families didn't have any kind of safety protections, and employers didn't cover occupational accidents and death.

Still, he didn't allow himself to be beaten by his past or the difficulties that plagued him during his life. On the contrary, he learned from these experiences and transformed them into the motivation to help other people. Chávez led a non-violent movement of awareness of and opposition to exploitation, and he founded the first union for the farm workers in the United States. The United Farm Workers of America fights racial and economic discrimination against Chicano residents and workers in general. Thanks to César Chávez, many agricultural workers, mostly poor immigrants, gained access to simple and basic rights, like a fair salary, bathrooms in the fields, drinking water, and break times for meals. It was also César Chávez who educated them on the dangers of the pesticides used on crops, which caused death and birth defects. Through his efforts, Chávez gave America and the rest of the world hope, inspiration, and education on the human rights of migrant laborers and workers in general.

His story has touched me deeply and has taught me that as a nation, we must do more to improve the quality of life and opportunities for education and health services among agriculture workers, whether they are here legally or illegally. I remember it daily, and I am constantly inspired by these words of the great César Chávez: "It is possible to become discouraged about the injustice we see everywhere. But God did not promise us that the world would be humane and just. He gives us the gift of life and allows us to choose the way we will use our limited time on earth. It is an awesome opportunity."

Nelson Mandela: Battle for freedom

Similar to Chávez, Nelson Mandela is another human being whom I deeply admire for the symbol of freedom that he represents to me and to millions of people all over the world. In 1994, Mandela became the first black man to become the President of South Africa and the first to be democratically chosen by both whites and blacks. He is a clear example of what a single person can achieve in his life through true dedication to a cause, the ability to forgive, and the willingness to free himself from the prisons that the past produces and to keep going despite all kinds of difficulties.

In early 1990, I met a mixed South African couple—the husband was white and the wife was black—who told me about their exile after facing racial discrimination and abuse daily for being an interracial couple. They explained that their relationship was considered illegal because of apartheid, a social system of racial segregation that existed in South Africa and Namibia, which was imposed by the white minorities until the 1991. Apartheid required separate housing, schools, and public areas and social events for blacks and whites. The white race had the exclusive power of voting, and marriages or sexual relations between whites and blacks were forbidden. The black race also lacked the power to move freely in their nation. This couple informed me that in their country, they couldn't live together, and if they decided to do so, they had to stay only in the black part of the community because the wife was not allowed in the white section.

Unfortunately, when they did move to the black section, the insults, disdain, rude comments, and discrimination persisted and even worsened. Their own families rejected them because of their union, and they couldn't even sit together on public transportation. The girl commented that, in time, her family members gradually accepted the situation, but her husband's family had stopped talking to him, preferring to disinherit him and even deny meeting their children, despite the fact that he was the only son. This story shook me because even if I knew that this happened in the United States until 1967, I had no idea that it existed in Africa until the 1990s! This kind of immigration based on racial persecution was new for me. I knew many people who had immigrated looking for a better future, including my own family, but these were the first immigrants whom I had met who came here just so that they could love someone of a different skin color. Such discrimination was completely unacceptable to me!

From a personal point of view, I was moved by the fact

that my husband and I are also from different races, and even though, thank God, we haven't had to endure any such discriminatory miseries, I couldn't help feeling great empathy for this couple who had been sentenced to exile from their homeland simply for loving one another and wanting to form a family together—a right that no one should be denied. Even if the exile cast a shade over this marriage, and even if the paternal family didn't know their grandchildren, the husband and wife both enthusiastically and happily followed in the steps of Nelson Mandela, who, immediately upon being released from prison, fought to end apartheid.

Mandela spent 27 years in prison because of his defense of black rights. Even while in jail, enduring subhuman conditions, Mandela was a free man inside himself, and he never stopped working for the cause. Neither sickness nor the low quality of life that he experienced during those years in captivity could break his spirit. The more I learned about Mandela, the more my admiration grew. I was so impressed by this man who didn't give up his freedom, even when he was sentenced to live in a prison for so many years. I wondered, where did his courage and faith come from? What was this individual's secret that enabled him to spend so much time locked up physically and still overcome the trauma of abuse, poor living conditions, and the torture that he both witnessed and received himself? His inner strength kept him going and allowed him to maintain impeccable dignity and human worth; it had to come from a greater source. I could understand this very well because I knew this source; it's the same one that also helped me to overcome my own traumatic events. He used forgiveness, generosity, compassion, and respect as his weapons of political persuasion, which proved to be more powerful than firearms or any sort of violence. And even after suffering years of imprisonment, once he was liberated, he didn't allow his sorrows and his pain to turn into bitterness, hatred, or a need for revenge. On the contrary, he taught his people tolerance and emphasized forgiveness to heal the wounds inflicted by racism. In doing so, he left a legacy of social unification, social ethnics, hope, and peace for black people in South Africa and for all races in the world, which has made him an icon in human history. Nelson Mandela said: "There is no easy walk to freedom anywhere, and many of us will have to pass through the valley of the shadow of death again and again before we reach the mountaintop of our desires."

Albert Einstein: The advantage of being different

As I mentioned before, upon coming to this country, I felt different for several reasons, and this caused me to become very quiet and reserved. Once, when I was talking about my fears with my advisor, she asked me if I was familiar with the life of Albert Einstein. Like most people, I only knew the basics: Einstein was a genius at mathematics, a subject that I have always found difficult to understand. My advisor then told me that even if he was a genius, when he was young, he was very quiet because people misunderstood his immense intellectual gifts, and he himself lacked the communication tools to help them understand.

Because of his withdrawn personality, he didn't have an easy childhood; he was a calm and imaginative child with slow intellectual development and low grades in school. His teachers believed that the young man had problems and that he wouldn't achieve much in life. His disdain for authority made him question conventional intelligence—though he was slow in verbal development, he was highly visual and thought in pictures instead of words. All of this drove him into a detailed exploration of time and space, subjects that are often taken for granted and which had not been scientifically explained with any adequacy at that time. Such peculiarities and limitations helped Einstein to find his inner motivation and to communicate in an entirely new way: through numbers and equations.

Hearing my advisor tell this story left quite the impression on me. I would´ve never thought that this genius physicist, mathematician, philosopher, and winner of a Nobel Peace Prize in Physics was ever labeled as having behavioral and learning problems. Who would've thought? Even if I have never considered myself a genius, I felt much more hopeful about my own history upon learning of Einstein's; even geniuses are underestimated. I am not alone.

His story continued to inspire me while I was employed as a social worker at a school. Many times, I met with extremely intelligent kids who had extraordinary qualities but were considered "problem kids." In some cases, they were given medication to help with their issues, but which may not have been necessary. I want to mention here that on occasion, a change in diet is enough, and the elimination of certain foods, like sugar, may modify "unusual" behavior in children, particularly hyperactivity. In this way, medicines and their side effects can be avoided, but this should be discussed with the child's physician first. When I was meeting with these types of children, I would tell them about

Einstein´s life, and they were as amazed as I was when I first heard it. They immediately opened up to me, and this enabled me to start working with them effectively.

Because many of these kids suffered from learning problems, they often dealt with academic challenges, which led to low self-esteem, isolation, depression, anxiety, and behavioral issues. Furthermore, failing in school gave them a disadvantage in relation to their classmates, who often separated them from the group and even mocked or physically abused them for being "stupid." Consequently, these children often didn't have many friends, and they had a hard time trusting people and respecting authority figures, like teachers, therapists, and parents, because they felt judged, singled out, and unfairly treated. Such circumstances may transform into a state of victimization, wherein the children feel powerless while facing problems, as they must work harder than their classmates to change their situation. They generally notice that everything seems easier for their classmates, and even though they make tremendous efforts to keep up with the pace of their class, they sometimes never achieve it. In addition, kids with learning problems frequently stay quiet, out of embarrassment or shame, because they believe that they are responsible for their situations, and so they deserve to "do bad," which becomes a type of punishment that they impose on themselves for being "less than" the rest of their classmates. This obviously fuels the problem and reinforces the negative vision that they have of themselves. In some cases, even when they are making progress, they still can't see it and are exhausted by "fighting in vain." Sometimes in school, even when they know the correct answers, they prefer to remain silent instead of possibly being mocked or misunderstood. In actuality, occasionally these kids have abilities that may have gone unnoticed, especially within the confines of conventional educational, but in other environments and with recognition from adults, they could excel.

Maybe a kid is slower to read or do mathematics than his classmates, but he is highly gifted in art or sports. Unfortunately, if these talents aren't recognized and encouraged, they run the risk of being forgotten or underutilized. The current educational system, in most countries, tends to overlook the innate gifts of "different" kids, while often guiding the parents and families down the wrong path for the treatment and ignoring the fact that they should help children to recognize their originality and make them feel appreciated and encouraged to keep on developing their potential to the fullest extent.

While doing social work, I was often inspired by Einstein's´ life and what I had learned from him regarding withholding judgment of people for their apparent disabilities, while also understanding that each one of us has something to contribute to society, regardless of intellectual or physical abilities. Each human being is born with a gift, and, if he is allowed to develop and express it, the whole world will benefit immensely. Humanity´s destiny wouldn't have been the same without Einstein´s contribution of the theory of relativity and the discoveries that then occurred in physics. Indeed, even my own work of giving hope and help to "special" kids and their families wouldn't have been the same if he hadn't existed.

Just like Einstein, many human beings have been judged, misunderstood, and occasionally abused for having abilities that seem lower than common intelligence, when in actuality they have something extremely special to offer the world. I believe that it is very important for parents to be able to recognize that even if their kids don't fit the current educational mold, it doesn't mean that they are "less entitled" to a full and happy life, or that they won't make a valuable contribution to society. If parents trust their children and offer them their unconditional support and love, then kids will learn to trust themselves. To close, I will share one of my favorite Albert Einstein´s quotes: "There is a driving force more powerful than steam, electricity and nuclear power: the will."

Bethany Hamilton: A good role model for young people

I am going to finish this annex by discussing a wonderful young woman who has not only deeply touched my heart, but also my teenager daughters'. In fact, my daughters are the ones who introduced me to Bethany Hamilton's life. They were fascinated by her story of faith, determination, will, and hope, and she has become a source of great inspiration for me as well. Hearing my daughters speak about Bethany was very touching for me because it opened an outlet through which I could share with them a little about what it meant to me to grow up without a role model to follow, or a mirror through which to ever imagine a better future. This conversation brought my daughters and me closer because we found a mutual comprehension that was new to the three of us.

It is common knowledge that good role models establish positive and necessary examples for teenage development while helping them to uncover the tools necessary to deal with the challenging influences and experiences that teenagers deal with as they grow up. Teenagers often consider movie stars, athletes, singers, and actors/actresses to be role models. However, it's important that teenagers also have role models with whom they can communicate through direct experience, such as teachers, coaches, classmates, elder brothers or sisters, and, of course, parents. While we grow, positive role models influence us and help us to visualize the path that we should follow, providing us with examples of how to behave when we are older. Having positive influences in their lives increases teenagers' possibilities of being successful and easily adapting to the different stages of adult life by opening doors to resolutions and choices that lead them to happiness.

Public figures like Bethany, who have overcome nearly impossible difficulties, are the perfect examples of positive influences in a teenager´s life. I hope that Bethany also acts as an example for you, no matter what age you are and no matter what you are going through in your life, because I want you to know that inside of you there is strength and wisdom that will help you to overcome your challenges and reach your dreams.

Bethany is an American surfer who was born into a surfer family in Hawaii. She started practicing the sport very young and began winning prizes and recognition in competitions. One Sunday, while my girls were at church during a youth service, the pastor brought up Bethany´s life, highlighting the way in which the girl overcame her difficulties that arose from an accident that she had when she was 13 and was attacked by a tiger shark while surfing with her friend. The pastor talked about how the attack had left Bethany without her left arm, and how she lost almost 60 percent of her blood. During her recovery, she endured several surgeries with an amazingly positive attitude and strength of spirit. Miraculously, a month after the attack, Bethany got back in the water and continued working toward her dream of becoming a professional surfer. Her return wasn't easy because she had to rehabilitate and learn to use her body in a new way. Surfing with just one arm was an immense challenge; however, she overcame the physical limitations and eventually became a surfing champion.

When the church service ended, my daughters kept talking about this girl's life and how faith in God helped her to recover. They were so inspired that they knew the whole story! Afterward, they made me run to the bookstore to buy Bethany Hamilton's biography so that we could read the book together and become even more familiar with the amazing events of this teenager's life—her bravery, her dedication to life, and her passion for surfing. I think it was the first time that I saw my daughters so excited about reading a book. The girls had just started taking surf lessons, and so they knew very well how hard it was to do it with all of their body parts intact. They couldn't even begin to imagine the great difficulty that Bethany encountered while using only one hand to push herself onto her feet and then balance her body in the ocean.

Bethany's life not only encouraged my daughters to hone their discipline when surfing; it also inspired them to overcome difficulties that may present themselves in other areas of their lives, like school and social relationships that can be very challenging in adolescence. In fact, I always bring her up when I see that they are struggling. I often tell them, "If Bethany could overcome her challenge, then you can deal with this." Many times, these are the only words that they need to hear to keep on going. They remember that even when Bethany had lost so much, she only thought of her recovery, without losing hope. She kept her faith firmly pinned to God and continued pursuing of her dreams.

I've seen the movie "Soul Surfer," which tells Bethany Hamilton's story. In fact, it became one of the favorite movies to watch at home, and I highly recommend that you see it with your children, parents, or loved ones because it is truly inspiring and will leave you with a feeling of courage, bravery, and hope about life. When thinking about her, I remember how important it is to have faith in God or in some superior force that provides us with the personal space in which to let everything out and then gather courage to overcome our challenges. I personally turn to God, but any source, like meditation or nature itself, may help; so too might another representation of the ubiquitous and omnipotent power of the Creator or the Universal Life Force. Whatever spirituality you adhere to can be there for you when you face life's obstacles.

The power of faith that helped Bethany to overcome her suffering is one of the most important creative forces and tools in existence. Faith is an energy that makes the fulfillment of "miracles" or unlikely events possible; without the help of this power, it would be impossible to achieve our dreams. "Faith moves mountains" and holds us in times of unhappiness and desperation. In fact, every book that is considered sacred speaks about the importance of having faith. Here I leave you with some examples:

- Now faith is the substance of things hoped for, the evidence of things not seen. Hebrews 11:1

- If ye have faith as a grain of mustard seed, ye shall say unto this mountain, Remove hence to yonder place; and it shall remove; and nothing shall be impossible unto you. Matthew 17:20

- The faith of all humans conforms to the nature of their mind. All people possess faith, and whatever the nature of their faith, that is verily what they are. Bhagavad Gita 17:3

- So lose not heart, nor fall into despair: For ye must gain mastery if ye are true in Faith. Qur'an 3:139

- On life's journey faith is nourishment… Buddha

You don't need to practice any specific religion to have faith, though doing so could help you to find it if have you lost faith. In truth, it is enough to establish contact with your spirit and with that Superior Strength that holds it; you can call it God, Jesus, Buddha, Muhammad, Jehovah, Divine Mother/Father, or whatever you like. What is important is that you know how to contact it, and that you have faith that it will help and support you during your process. This was the great lesson that I learned from Bethany Hamilton. Since learning about her, I have followed her life through her speeches, books, and movies. One of her quotes that I always have present is, "I don't need easy, I just need possible."

ACKNOWLEDGEMENTS

I want to express my most sincere acknowledgment to several colleagues, family members, and friends who have helped me to finish this book. Without their support and guidance, this book wouldn't have been possible.

To my husband and daughters, for their support, affection, and unconditional love.

To my mother, for all of the effort and the sacrifices that you made to give me a better future.

To my late father, for helping to give me life, which is the most precious gift in the world.

To my brothers, because they are part of my journey through life, which has taught me so much.

To my advisor at George Washington High School, Ms. Rodríguez, whose invaluable help, support, and patience helped me to grow personally and professionally.

To New Paltz University, for giving me the chance to make a better future for myself, and also for being the place where I met my husband and best friend.

To all of the doctors who cared for me during my illness, specially my holistic healer, who pushed me to heal from the inside out.

To my friends, who were so supportive in this process. You know who you are because I consider you angels that God sent me in this life.

To my clients, who gave me the chance to help.

To God, for filling my life with blessings.

To those of you who are reading this book, for believing in me and supporting me.

All my love and sincere gratitude.

BIBLIOGRAPHY

Adler, R., Felten, D.L., Cohen, N.,
Psychoneuroimmunology, Second Edition. USA:
Academic Press 1991.

American Academy of Pediatrics. Girls are Beginning
Puberty at a Younger Age. 9 de Agosto, 2010. aap.org

American Academy of Pediatrics: Stresses of single
parenting (2007). healthychildren.org

American College of Rheumatology. Exercise and
arthritis. rheumatology.org

American Heart Association. About sodium (salt).
heart.org. 29 de Abril 2014

American Psychological Association. Parenting: being
supermom stressing you out? apa.org

Bartlett, S., Moonaz, S., Bernatsky, S. Yoga in rheumatic

diseases. Complementary and Alternative Medicine: Current Rheumatology Reports. 15 (2013) 387

Bayego, Enric., Vila, Gemma., Martinez, Inigo. Prescripción de ejercicios físico: indicaciones, posología, y efectos adversos. Medicina Clinica, 138 (2012) 18-24

Beaulieu-Presley, P., Harmon, S. Elvis and Me. USA: Penguin Putnam Inc. 1986

Berman, Marc., Jonides, John., Kaplan, Stephen. The cognitive benefits of interacting with nature. Journal of Psychological Science, 19 (2008) 1207-1212

Beth, M., Lesowitz, N. Living Life as a Thank You. The transformational power of daily gratitude. USA: Metro Book. 2009

Bilban, Martin. Human but Not Mouse Adipogenesis Is Critically Dependent on LMO3. Journal of Cell Metabolism. 18 (2013) 62-74

Campdelacreu, Jaume. Enfermedad de Parkinson y enfermedades de Alzheimer: Factores de riesgo ambientales. Neurologia 29 (2014) 541-549

Cattaneo, Annamaria., Macchi, Flavia., Plazzotta, Giona., Berican, Begni., Bocchio Chiavetto, Luisella.,

Riva, Marco., Pariante, Carmine. Inflammation and neuronal plasticity: a link between childhood trauma and depression pathogenesis. Journal of Frontiers in Cellular Neuroscience, 9: 40 (2015)

Center for Disease Control and Prevention. Get the facts: sodium and the dietary guidelines. cdc.gov

Cereda, Emanuele., Pezzoli, Gianni. Exposure to pesticides or solvents and risks of Parkinson disease. Journal of the American Academy of Neurology. 80 (2013) 2035-2041.

Chizuru Nishida., Uauy, Ricardo. WHO scientific update on health consequences of trans-fatty acids: introduction. European Journal of Clinical Nutrition. 63 (2009) 1–4.

Columbia University Medical Center. Perceived stress may predict future risk of coronary heart disease. newsroom.cumc.columbia.edu. 17 de Diciembre, 2012

Collis, Helen. "Food Really Is Addictive: Study Finds Brain Activity Similar to Heroin Users after Eating Certain Processed Foods." *Daily Mail Online*. Associated Newspapers, 27 June 2013.

Dr. Mercola. "Alimentos saludables que nunca, nunca deberías comer." espanol.mercola.com., 04 de Octubre

2011

Drexler, Peggy. "Why there are more walk-away moms" cnn.com. 6 de Mayo, 2013

Duke, James, PH.D. The Green Pharmacy Guide to Healing Foods: Proven natural remedies to treat and prevent more than 80 common health concerns. USA: Rodale Inc, 2008.

Duke Today. Increased fructose consumption may deplete cellular energy in patients with obesity and diabetes. today.duke.edu. 2 de Mayo, 2012

Eaton, John. "Que son las endorfinas."? reverse-therapy.es

ElBoghdady, Dina. Judge orders FDA to revisit decision not to ban some antibiotics in animal feed. washingtonpost.com. 5 de Junio, 2012.

Emmons, Robert., Mccullough, M. Counting blessings versus burdens: An experimental investigation of gratitude and subjective well-being in daily life. Journal of Personality and Social Psychology, 84 (2003) 377-389

European Commission. Press Release Database. Growth promoting hormones pose health risk to consumers, confirms EU scientific committee. Brussels.

23 de Abril 2002. europa.eu

Ferdman, Robert. Why pepsi's decision to ditch aspartame isn't good for soda or science. washingtonpost.com. 27 de Abril, 2015.

Fernando, Cesareo. El estrés en las enfermedades cardiovasculares. Libro de la Salud Cardiovascular del Hospital Clínico San Carlos y la Fundación BBVA. Fundacion BBVA. Espana. (2009) Capítulo 66, 583-520

Fox, Kenneth. The influence of physical activity on mental well-being. Public Health Nutrition, 2 (1999) 411-418

Gallagher, James., Salir a caminar puede ser clave para curar la depresión.bbc.com., 29 de Abril 2012

Garcia-Rios, Antonio., Meneses, Maria., Perez-Martinez Pablo., Perez-Jimenez Francisco. Omega-3 y enfermedad cardiovascular: más allá de los factores de riesgo. Nutrición Clinica y Dietética Hospitalaria. 29 (2009) 4-16

Geoghegan, Tom. "Who, What, Why: How Long Is the Ideal Nap?" *BBC News*. BBC, 29 Apr. 2011.

Harvard Health Publications. The gut-brain connection. view.mail.health.harvard.edu.27 de Marzo, 2012.

Hoffman, Paul. Meditar mientras caminas.
blog.omsica.com

Instituto de Medicina del Sueño. La importancia de
dormir bien. dormirbien.info

Instituto de Investigación y Salud. La importancia de
estar bien hidratados.institutoaguaysalud.es

John Hopkins Bloomberg School of Public Health.
Study suggests home cooking is a main ingredient in
healthier diet. 17 de Noviembre, 2014. jhsph.edu

Kashdan, Todd., Uswatte, Gitendra., Julian, Terri.
Gratitude and hedonic and eudaimonic well-being in
Vietnam war veterans. Journal of Behaviour Research
and Therapy, 44 (2006) 177-199.

Kim, Susanna. 11 foods ingredients banned outside the
U.S. that we eat.abcnews.go.com. 26 de Junio, 2013.

Kobylewski, S., Jacobson, F. Food dyes a rainbow of
risks. Center for Science in the Public Interest. 2010.
cspinet.org

Konturek, PC., Brzozowski, T., Konturek, SJ. Stress
and the gut: Pathophysiology, clinical consequences,
diagnostic approach and treatment options. Journal of
Physiology and Pharmacology. 69 (2011) 591-599

Korb, Alex. The Grateful Brain. psychologytoday.com 20 de Noviembre, 2012

Lamb, Trisha. Health benefits of yoga. The International Association of Yoga Therapists.iayt.org

Lee, I-Min., Buchner, David. The importance of walking to public health:, Journal of Medicine and Science in Sports and Exercise 40 (2008) : S 512-8

Martínez, R., El Agua Mineral Natural: Una bebida esencial en nuestra hidratación. Informe Científico de Instituto de Investigación Agua y Salud. 2 Septiembre del 2010

Medrano, Ivan. Actividad de los músculos para vertebrales durante ejercicios que requieran estabilidad raquídea. Universidad de Valencia: Departamento de Educación Física y Deportiva (2011): 1-218

Morales, Tatiana. Inflammation linked to heart illnesses. 14 de Noviembre, 2002.cbsnews.com.

Mooney, Andrea. This is your brain on a high-glycemic diet. Boston's Children's Science and Clinical Innovation Blog. 28 de Junio del 2013. vector.childrenshospital.org.

Mozaffarian, Dariush., Fahimi, Saman., Singh,

Gitanjali., Micha, Renata., Khatibzadeh, Shahab., Engell, Rebecca., Stephen, Lim., Goodarz, Danaei., Majid, Ezzati., Powles, John. Global sodium consumption and death from cardiovascular causes. The New England Journal of Medicine. 371 (2014) 624-634.

Murray, N.D., Pizzorno, Joseph. The encyclopedia of natural medicine. Third edition.New York: Atria, 2012.

Murphy, M., and S. Donovan. The physiological and psychological effects of meditation: A review of contemporary research with a comprehensive bibliography *1931-1996*. Second edition. California: The institute of Noetic Sciences. 1997.

Nair, Rathish., Maseeh, Arun. Vitamin D: the "sunshine" vitamin. Journal of Pharmacology and Pharmacotherapy. 3 (2012) 118-126.

Organización Mundial de la Salud. Dieta, Nutrición y Prevención de Enfermedades Crónicas. Informe de una Consulta Mixta de Expertos. Ginebra: Organización Mundial de la Salud, 2003.

Organización Mundial de la Salud. Estrategia mundial sobre régimen alimentario, actividad física y salud: Fomento del consumo mundial de frutas y verduras.

2002. who.int/en/

Organización Mundial de la Salud. Que es la diabete?
who.int/diabetes/action_online/basics/es/

Organización Mundial de la Salud. Resistencia a los
antimicrobianos: Una amenaza mundial. Boletín de
Medicamentos Esenciales. 28 y 29, (2000) 7-19

Physicians Committee for Responsible Medicine. Foods
for cancer prevention. pcrm.org

Raloff, Jane. Hormones: here is the beef.
Environmental concerns reemerge over steroids give to
livestock. Science News, 161 (1), (2002)

Rosekind, Mark., Smith, Roy., Miller, Donna., Co,
Elizabeth., Gregory, Kevin., Webbon, Lisa., Gander,
Philippa. Alertness management: strategic naps in
operational settings. Journal of Sleep Research. 4 suppl.
2 (1995) 62-66

Sanitas Más Salud. La fibra en la prevención de la
obesidad. sanitas.es

Sociedad Argentina de Medicina del Estrés. Relación
entre el estrés emocional y la hipertensión arterial.
www. same.org

Stohr, Klaus. Resistencia a los antimicrobianos. Problemas del uso de antimicrobianos en la agricultura y la ganadería. Boletín de Medicamentos Esenciales. Número 28 y 29 (2000) 10-12. apps.who.int

Stump, Scott. Nap rooms encourage sleeping on the job to boost productivity. 15 de Marzo del 2013. today.com.

Sunkaria, Ramesh., Kumar, Vinod., Suresh, Chandra. A comparative study on spectral parameters of heart rate variability in yogi and non-yogic practitioners. Journal of Medical Engineering and Informatics. 2 (2010) 1-14

Team Hoyt. Yes You Can! teamhoyt.com

University of California Television. Sugar: The Bitter Truth. 27 de Julio, 2009. uctv.tv United States Food and Drug Administration. FDA cuts *Trans* Fat in processed foods. 16 de Junio, del 2015. fda.gov

Walker, Matthew., Mander, Byce., Santhanam, Saletin. Wake deterioration and sleep restoration of human learning. Current Biology, 21 (2011) 183-184

WallJasper, Jay. Walking as a way of life: Movement for health and happiness.everybodywalk.org.

Ware, Bronnie. The top five regrets of the dying. 1ro de

Luz Avila-Kyncl

Febrero, 2012. the guardian.com.

Winter, R. A Consumer's Dictionary of Food Additives.
Descriptions in plain english of more than 12,000
ingredients both harmful and desirable found in foods.
USA: Three Rivers Press. 2004

Made in the USA
San Bernardino, CA
09 August 2017